D0918286

THE DIMENSIONALITY OF
SIGNS, TOOLS, AND MODELS

ADVANCES IN SEMIOTICS
General Editor, Thomas A. Sebeok

THE DIMENSIONALITY OF
Signs, Tools, and Models

An Introduction

by JAMES H. BUNN

INDIANA UNIVERSITY PRESS

BLOOMINGTON

Copyright © 1981 by James H. Bunn

All rights reserved

No part of this book may be reproduced or utilized in any form
or by any means, electronic or mechanical, including photocopying
and recording, or by any information storage and retrieval system,
without permission in writing from the publisher. The Association
of American University Presses' Resolution on Permissions constitutes
the only exception to this prohibition.

Manufactured in the United States of America

Library of Congress Cataloging in Publication Data

Bunn, James H   1938-
　The dimensionality of signs, tools, and models.

　(Advances in semiotics)
　Includes bibliographical references and index.
　1.Semiotics.　I.Title.　II.Series.
P99.B85 001.51 80–8151
ISBN 0–253–16916–X　1 2 3 4 5 85 84 83 82 81

To Frances Middelton Bunn

Contents

PREFACE

This study began in a classroom where I was trying to explain a curious pattern. Readers of English novels might remember in *Tristram Shandy* how Uncle Toby began to ride his hobby horse. He was wounded in the groin at the siege of Namur, and his convalescence was impeded because none of his well-wishing visitors could understand the military jargon of siege warfare, which Uncle Toby deployed when they asked where he had been wounded. Uncle Toby was too modest to point to a section of his own anatomy, so he expediently tried to locate just where he had fallen at Namur. Then he was given a map by his brother, who grieved at Uncle Toby's vexatious inability to communicate. The aid of a map worked so well that Uncle Toby ordered as many other maps as there were campaigns; whereupon his hobby of siege warfare began in and for itself. His health improved wonderfully at his servant's suggestion that they go down to the country and build in the garden an actual earthworks model of the fortification. Lawrence Sterne's madcap novel about the way innocent pursuits of knowledge become displaced into grooved ruling passions is part of an eighteenth-century preoccupation, which is also ours; it is about how practical means to a desired end become twisted into a pleasurable end in itself.

But there was further distortion in Uncle Toby's case. His single-minded preoccupation with building actual earthworks models of fortress cities reversed the tendency toward stylization in a historical process. For the jargon of counterscarps, demi-bastions, half-moons, ravelins, had become so abstract that Uncle Toby reverted to a two-dimensional pictograph and then to a three-dimensional model composed of miniature cannon and bridge. What are the relative merits of dimensionality as one shifts kinds of discourse in order to approximate the thing itself? Is there some kind of means-ends confusion at the very heart of discourse? What are the consequences for discovery of these shifts in dimensionality and in intent?

The present study introduces the ways that any instrument works according to its dimensional limits. I have followed Uncle Toby's hobby horse and have divided the chapters so they correspond with the several Euclidean dimensions. The first chapter concerns three-dimensional signs, tools, and models as they exist 'in the round'; the second chapter explores two-dimensional pictographs such as maps and graphs; the third chapter outlines some basics of one-dimensional signs that work in time; and the fourth chapter explores models that are apparently 'whole systems'.

My premise is that every conceptual tool, each abstract model, or any piece of hardware that the minds of humans might imagine, will occupy those basic dimensions that all of us experience and most of us can comprehend. So by devoting an individual chapter to each of the several dimensions, we can provide a practical grammar for approaching all instruments in common. But we shall not be concerned with the many different kinds of signs, tools, and models extant in diverse trades; instead we need to measure the ways in which any instrument works according to its dimensional limits. Then the study might serve as a primer, as a primary entrance, to the more complicated problem of how one begins to probe the world. Perhaps the most useful first step in that regard is my arrangement of human thought into six categories. In the introductory chapter, signs, tools, and models are divided into six kinds of instruments, because that number exhausts the dimensional possibilities of our artificial extensions.

Dimensional signs intercede for us in discovering the new. Yet this is not so much a study of *how* one discovers, as it is a primer which categorizes instruments one discovers *with*. For signs, tools, and models are nothing other than artificial substitutes that we use for probing practical and theoretical problems that are not yet satisfactorily resolved. The study therefore introduces the dimensions of probing, because in all disciplines discovery depends upon conjecture about a hypothetical problem that has been articulated in one or more of these artificial dimensions.

Throughout the book we shall continue to ask a primary question about the nature of discovery: What are the means and ends of our discourses? Early in the Introduction, for instance, we shall see that a shift in means and ends is an integral of ritualized signaling among animals. We must also use means-ends conversions to discuss shifts from utilitarian to esthetic aims, and from tool making to model building; and finally, in the Conclusion we shall observe that for a number of thinkers, including Einstein and Heidegger, a means-ends reversal has been responsible for rendering technology into an instrumental fetish that defines some contemporary misvalues. Uncle Toby's dilemma about means and ends was less innocent than was his own character.

Now let me mention the method or machinery which drives this book. In general, I have derived it from the figure-ground relationship of Gestalt psychology. Every three-dimensional object that we employ or examine as a sign must be considered as a figural element in its environmental ground. What is the palace at Versailles without its landscape gardens? Similarly, a two-dimensional image is meaningful only in relation to the flat plane that helps organize it. And a one-dimensional sign is meaningful only in relation to the temporal sequence in which it is enscrolled with other signs in the series. So the method is useful if only because it has allowed me to express the dimensional limits of signs in six figure-ground variations.

I must admit, too, that there is a theoretical bias to my method. Although I have read with diligence and with respect those writers who are grouped together as the French structuralists, I have for the most part ignored their more recent work. My reasons are primarily thematic: this is a study of the way that signs, tools, and models intercede for us in the process of discovery. But, crassly put, their preoccupation is almost entirely with the duplicitous quality of language and with its harmful constraints upon action. Let me quickly add that theirs continue to be incisive works. Their central text in this regard is E. A. Poe's "Purloined Letter," wherein a letter is turned inside out, deceptively misaddressed, and so serves as a seminal text for fictive sleight of hand. So I tend to use, somewhat eclectically, Anglo-American writers about signs—ranging from Thomas Hobbes to C. S. Peirce—who tend to be more utilitarian and pragmatic about semiotic intervention in the world. In the conclusion of this study, however, I try to resolve the main ambiguities of alienation that result from "my" kind of instrumentalist view, where all objects are seen to be exploitable for transfer to some other use.

With regard to the process of discovery I am very much indebted to the works of Rudolf Arnheim, Gerald Holton, Michael Polanyi, and Karl R. Popper. A more extensive citation will appear in the text, but it would be inappropriate to ignore their extremely important explorations. At various times as I have careened this study, a number of people have challenged, guided, or encouraged me; notably, Gale Carrithers, Angus Fletcher, Lejaren Hiller, Irving Massey, Joseph Riddel, Fred See. Anthony J. Rozak transformed my working sketches into accomplished models of visual thinking. Hilda Ludwig patiently typed an unwieldy manuscript. Some of the photographs were taken at the Educational Communications Center, State University of New York at Buffalo. The preparation of the illustrations was aided by a grant from the Julian Park Fund of the State University of New York at Buffalo. Finally, this book owes much to its setting: the rich, intellectual anarchy of the Buffalo English Department.

THE DIMENSIONALITY OF
SIGNS, TOOLS, AND MODELS

Introduction

In beginning, let us make an agreement about our words. Let us begin to define signs, tools, and models by way of a mutual agreement. So let us understand 'agreement'. Most fairy tales, you will remember, begin with an agreement that becomes more complicated as the story develops. In "The Frog Prince," for instance, a lovely princess by mistake dropped her golden ball down a well in the forest. Her need then gave rise to a wish, when a frog rose out of the well. "What will you give me if I retrieve your ball?" he said. "I will promise you anything," she said, "if only you will bring back my golden ball." So the princess agreed to take up the frog, to allow him henceforth to eat from her plate, and to sleep in her bed. The appearance in fairy tales of this kind of 'if-then' contract, where mutual lack is turned into mutual profit, is perhaps one of the earliest experiences we learn as children about that curious state of mutual responsibility in which a hypothetical idea, a fiction, a fantasy, is enjoined to become a reality.

In "The Frog Prince" the lesson is highlighted by the princess' wish to avoid the consequences of her agreement. For we recall that she ran away from the frog once he had retrieved the ball, but her father, the King, enforced the agreement by saying that we must all keep our word. A word is a promise about a future. The tale is rightly admired for its interweaving of nature and culture. Her lack or need in the deep woods of nature is matched by the frog's analogous appetite; their contract is a mutual transfer of rights, for which the golden ball is but a token, a diminished sign of the more important future state, where the frog will be transformed utterly into a cultured handsome prince, and where they will live together happily ever after.

Let us now examine our agreement more closely. The fairy tale allows us to infer that fairy tales reverse the order of means and ends. Just as hunger envisions a sumptuous meal, so in the order of desire at large a fantasy or vision about the future precedes the means of implementing that end in the 'real' world. Any agreement is a fantasy wherein the future precedes and overrides the present. So the "future" is for the student of signs, as it was for Thomas Hobbes, "but a fiction of the mind, applying the sequels of actions past to the actions that are present."[1] Hobbes was the originator of modern semiotics, the study of signs, just as he was the master of contracts. Both signs and contracts are fictions about the future. In Hobbes' view the best "prophet" is the best "guesser" about signs:

> A sign is the event antecedent of the consequent; and contrarily, the consequent of the antecedent, when the like consequences have been observed before: And the oftener they have been observed, the less uncertain is the sign (p. 11).

So for Hobbes, clouds are signs of impending rain, and rain is a sign of clouds past. It is apparent from this passage that for Hobbes the repetition of contiguous events in nature gives rise to the probability that the series may be read as a sign, that there is agreement between antecedent and consequent. So the idea of discovery is the probability of uncovering signs of agreement. In nature one looks for and discovers signs of agreement; in culture one invents antecedent agreements as the basis for signs.

Hobbes uses the peculiarly modern word, "conjecture," to describe this process of discovering antecedents.[2] Imagination, fantasy, hunches, intuitions, conjectures, are words we use for the processes of discovery. In this sense fantasies or fairy tales are conjectures that the world makes about its structural agreements. Design is the desire of the world. For as Hobbes said, "From Desire, ariseth the Thought of some means we have seen produce the like of that which we aim at . . ." (p. 9). So we construct a fiction about the future based upon prior agreement between antecedents and consequences that we remember from nature.

Conjectures about antecedents and consequences are the radical bases of all 'if-then' agreements, whether in nature or in social contracts. If a sign is an event "antecedent of its consequent," as well as its reversal, we may initially define a sign in a Hobbesian manner: A sign is the radical of social contract. This definition is simplicity itself, even to the point of grotesquery, because everyone has already agreed to it in practice. Recall, for instance, that scene in *A Midsummer Night's Dream* where the Athenian rustics are rehearsing their version of the tragedy of Pyramus and Thisbe. They hope to present the play at the festivities following the wedding of Theseus and Hippolyta, but being innocent of theatrical custom, they fear their audience will be unable to discriminate betwixt illusion and reality. Snug the joiner is to play the lion, but Bottom the weaver fears that a lion among the ladies of the audience will be too fearful to behold. So they agree to "let him name his name, and tell them plainly he is Snug the joiner." A more difficult crux is the wall that separates the estates of Pyramus and Thisbe. Bottom decides as before: "Some man or other must present Wall; and let him have some plaster, or some loam, or some roughcast about him to signify wall; or let him fold his fingers thus, and through that cranny shall Pyramus and Thisbe whisper." Toward the end of the play the rustics' little play about theatrics is played exactly as they had desired, with Snout the tinker standing for Wall. After he has recited his speech about signifying wall, one of the characters in the audience says, "It is the wittiest partition that ever I heard discourse."

The wonderful simplicity of Shakespeare's art is nicely set forth in this little comedy about Wall. Signs are the primordial agreement, for the understanding of a semiotic code binds two (or more) people in a set of tacitly agreed upon conventions about what stands for what. In making the contract about Wall explicit, by drawing attention to the invisible "partition" between illusion and reality, Shakespeare reminds us that a word is both conduit and boundary. It "discourses," but it also separates and connects two lovers; it is the radical of mediation. For Wall is a distinction. By drawing attention to its difference, Bottom exposes the very machinery of theatrical fantasy as well as the machinery of contracts. All contracts are intercessions, walls, between two or more people that displace an agreement into a third 'thing', a sign.

Let Snout represent Wall. Each separate entity exchanges characteristics with the other; the result is a displaced third thing, a grotesque sign. All along, we have tacitly agreed that those black, squiggly marks, $W A L L$, together signify a three-dimensional boundary; but if we were in Shakespeare's audience, we would see antecedent and consequent come together in a grotesquely explicit sign when Snout represents Wall at the end of the larger play. Signs are complicated variations upon a simple theme of exchange with displacement, the pattern of 'if-then'. For signs involve both temporal and spatial exchanges. Bottom's desire not to terrify the ladies is a conjecture, a fiction, about the future of his play. Signs exchange, by reversing, the ordinary pattern of past, present, future; because signs, as we shall see in Chapter 3, are always involved with expectant usage. Desire enjoins the future to become actual via the magic of signs. If signs reverse temporality by making the future seem to come before the present means, then in addition they exchange characteristics spatially, as with the wall that separates Pyramus and Thisbe. As we shall see throughout this book, signs, tools, and models of discovery are strange hybrids that exist 'in' a grotesque hypothetical dimension which re-presents 'real' time and space.

Further along in this introduction, we shall arrive at more precise definitions of signs, tools, and models. But consider momentarily the reflective qualities of a model of discovery in this context of semiotic reversals. A model is something that we construct in order to predict the characteristics of a large problem whose nature we do not yet understand. The paradox of model building is that models also reverse the order of time's arrow by imaginatively incorporating the future in a fictive construct. Dr. Frankenstein's model turned out subsequently to be a monster; he imagined for it a handsome future. In literary theory such fictive models are called 'doubles'. They re-present reality with a slight difference. So models of discovery are similar to doubles in literary theory in the sense that both mediate between the fictive and the real. We imagine a future state by incorporating a model that reflects those imaginary dimensions in three space. The logic for this kind of mediation is again elementary: signs, we have said, mediate between the past and the future by seeming to incorporate in themselves both antecedent and consequent. And desire prompts our conjectures about signs. For instance, Elie Halevy once made in another context a Hobbeslike statement, "Exchange is the simplest and most typical of all social phenomena; it is the original cause of the harmony of egoisms."[3] Desire prompts exchange, whether of commodities in space, or of contracts about the future. Exchange and reversal are the same phenomenon, with one viewed from a spatial and the other from a temporal perspective. This study is perspectivist throughout, for the six categories of instruments are simply six different ways of turning and viewing objects. Here we can stipulate that exchange and reversal are therefore radicals of semiotic agreement.

Let us also stipulate that this kind of if-then agreement about a conjectural future occurs 'in' a fictive dimension, separate from, but similar to, the 'real' world to which it refers. When Daedalus grafted wings onto the body of his son and agreed with him about the dangers of their use, Icarus leapt to his peril into a dimension that is more symbolic than the space of ground dwellers. Those Daedalian wings belong to a class of artificial limbs that include all signs, tools, and models of discovery. Semiotics is the study of that class; it is the study of signs, their artifice, as well as their mediation. And the arena 'in' which they operate and to which they refer is the semiotic dimension, the hypothetical state of things.[4] If signs, tools, and models serve as daemons that transcend the limitations of here and now, the semiotic dimension is nonetheless reached by instruments that are forged from wax, feathers, and other mundane stuff. So the Daedalian artifice that extends our conditional limits is a winged boundary between the stuff of nature and the operations of culture. Consider that a sign, tool, or model can be initially defined as some material thing, enjoined to change from one category of use and to stand in for a new task. Because all instruments probe a fictive or hypothetical dimension different from their physical dimensions, they seem to exhibit a bootstrap principle of *palingenesis*, of drawing back to a more primitive state in order to leap or to fly to a higher. As Paul Watzlawick says of the theory of logical types, ". . . going from one level to the next higher (i.e., from member to class) entails a shift, a jump, a discontinuity or transformation—in a word, a change—of the greatest theoretical and therefore practical importance, for it provides a way *out of* a system."[5] Hence, a first rule of our study is that any human artifact will retain vestiges of its physical origin as it is discontinuously yoked to a new task, and therefore that all signs, tools, and models in practice will seem to have leapt to the new dimension. Conjectural leaps via semiotic discourse will be an important part of this study; leaps are metaphors for "by way of."

Animal
Communication

There is good reason to use the evolutionary term of palingenesis, because animals other than *homo faber* apparently use symbolic communication by way of palingenesis, and there is ample evidence for suggesting that human semiotics evolved in ways similar to the evolutionary patterns of other animals. In his classic essay "Courtship-Habits of the Great Crested Grebe" Julian Huxley pioneered inquiry about symbolic communication among animals.[6] Furthermore, his use of the term "ritualization" effectively defined the semiotic transfer between categories that makes all symbols seem discontinuous. In that essay he observed among grebes a displacement of their common habits, such as preening and aggression, into the semiotic dimension of their mating ceremony. The most spectacular part of their courtship dance is a segment in which both male and female dive and emerge with a beak full of weed. They then rapidly approach each other and leap from the water; by paddling furiously, they stand mutually erect (see Figure 1). Huxley observed that this and other parts of the dance originally served as a useful action, which then turned into a symbol, and subsequently into a ritual: "or, in other words, the change by which the same act which first served a definite purpose directly comes later to subserve it only indirectly (symbolically), and then not at all" (506). For example, the physical act of ascending the nest and of assuming a passive attitude for coition is first used by either in the dance on the open water "as a sign of the readiness to pair":

> We may say that readiness to pair is indicated precociously—it is pushed back a step. Such processes of pushing back are very common in early ontogeny; embryologists then say that the time of the appearance of the character is *coeno-genetic* (even though the character itself, as here, may be palingenetic). The phylogenetic change

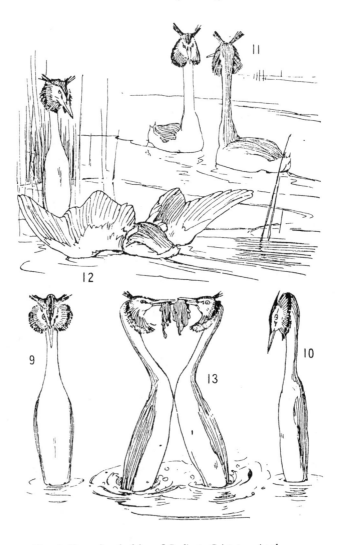

Fig. 1. Courting habits of *Podiceps Cristatus.* At the center of the sketch is the most dramatic part of the western grebes' courtship ritual, where the partners rise into a "penguin dance." From Julian Huxley, "The Courtship Habits of the Great Crested Grebe," *Proceedings of the Zoological Society of London.*

has here been precisely similar; the only difference is that the displacement affects a mature instead of a very early period of life (p. 507).

There is a null point in this diachronic process. For grebes repeat this passive attitude in the open water, one with another, and then resume their ordinary acts of preening or feeding:

> From useful symbolism to mere ritual is the last step—one that has taken place often enough in various human affairs. It appears that these actions and attitudes, once symbolic of certain states of mind and leading up to certain definite ends, lose their active symbolism and become ends in themselves (p. 507).

This semiotic pattern of exchange with displacement, which Huxley called ritualization, has subsequently become a serviceable concept for other ethologists' understanding of animal communication. Edward O. Wilson has explained that ritualized symbols emerge among animals when they are in conflict about how to complete an act.[7] Their hesitant behavior about a course of action is communicated to other animals of the same species and so comes to signal the possible need to coordinate activity in the group. Many species of birds have ritualized a hesitancy, about whether or not to fly, into a crouching stance that signals a warning to others. This semiotic dimension works by virtue of logical types. Signaling depends upon the class of birds that defines its members, but it is of a different category of meaning than the ritualized crouching in preparation to leap of an individual bird. Only as it is a member of the group do the physical acts take on symbolic meaning.

Increasing degrees of ritualization among individual species provide important steps for understanding the evolution of communication displays among neighboring species. Wilson offers an instructive example of several species of dance flies that have similar courtship displays (p. 35). In one species the courtship merely involves a simple approach by the male, but in another species the male offers another insect to his carnivorous partner, apparently in order to escape falling victim himself. In still another species the male attaches threads of silk to the insect, "rendering it more distinctive in appearance, a clear step in the direction of ritualization." And another species completely encloses the offering. Some decrease the offering but maintain the size of the cocoon. Finally, "the male of another species does not bother to capture any prey object but simply offers the female an empty balloon" (p. 35).

This kind of displacement of aggression into a semiotic dimension, by means of increasing ritualization, prompted Konrad Lorenz to follow his colleague Huxley's example and to use it as an equation for human ritual or art:[8] "There is hardly a doubt that all human art primarily developed in the service of rituals and that the autonomy of 'art for art's sake' was achieved only by another secondary step of cultural progress" (p. 73). This telescoping of culture into nature achieves its allure by way of a similar semiotic pattern. Although Lorenz's line of development will not be followed here, one can seize upon the pattern of means-ends variation in order to understand better the hypothetical dimension that is pointed to. For many human rituals, as well as tools and models, have bionic origins.

Presently, one of these rites, the crane dance, will be explored, but first consider more closely the ritualization among dance flies of that empty cocoon. Wilson states that this display "is so far removed from the original behavior pattern that its evolutionary origin in this empid species might have remained a permanent mystery if biologists had not discovered what appears to be the full story of its development preserved step by step in the behavior of related species" (pp. 35–36). Instead of using the empty balloon as a model for evolution among dance flies or of using it as a model for the development of human ritual and art, let us use it as an analogy for understanding the hypothetical dimension of semiosis. It might also be used by some structuralist followers of the anthropologist Claude Lévi-Strauss to argue an essentially deceptive quality in communication, the argument being that the sign deceives as much as it communicates by diverting attention from the true state of affairs.[9] Or a Marxist literary theorist like G. Lukacs might maintain that as a commodity it has become fetishized by a process of reification.[10] Those arguments will be noticed in subsequent chapters, for there exists an essential means-ends confusion in semiotic functions that must be clarified if discovery is to work.

In the context of the dance fly's empty balloon, the end point of ritualization is a complete destruction of the material object from which it began. It is the extreme of parsimony in that natural series. By understanding the evolution of the series, one conceives the empty container to represent a type for the species. Now by a similar process of extrapolation C. S. Peirce explained in *Speculative Grammar* that the linguistic sign, a "symbol," refers not to an object but rather to a general class. As Roman Jakobson summarizes in an influential essay, "a symbol, for instance, a word, is a 'general rule' which signifies only through the different instances of its application. . . ."[11] Although a "table" may be used to refer to a specific object in the room, as a sign it still refers to the whole class. In effect Peirce emptied the sign of all its material members, making it a type different from all its specific usages. By means of a similar logic, Peirce maintained that mathematics is not a study of quantities of objects, but rather it is "the study of what is true of hypothetical states of things":

> For all modern mathematicians agree with Plato and Aristotle that mathematics deals exclusively with hypothetical states of things, and asserts nothing of fact whatever; and further that it is thus alone that the necessity of its conclusions is to be explained.[12]

For Whitehead also, mathematics is the penultimate logical type: "Mathematics is thought moving in the sphere of complete abstraction from any particular instance of what it is talking about."[13] Like the empty balloon, at its extreme the hypothetical dimension of semiotics is similarly emptied of all its specific occasions and natural dimensions. And like any other class without members it becomes a null set.

The extreme of this kind of thinking is Ferdinand de Saussure's conception of *la langue*, which is "the sum of the verbal images stored up in all the individuals, a treasure deposited by the practice of speaking in the members of a given community; a grammatical system, virtually existing in each brain, or more exactly in the brains of a body of individuals; for *la langue* is not complete in any one of them, it exists in perfection only in the mass."[14] Odgen and Richards attack this as a "fantastic" notion, one that could only be arrived at by some "Method of Intensive Distraction analogous to that with which Dr. Whitehead's name is associated." Whitehead's Fallacy of Misplaced Concreteness will be explored in Chapter 3.

In view of the logical dangers of extrapolation, I agree with Rudolf Arnheim that linguistic signs must be linked with percepts of different dimensions if discovery is to result.[15] For Arnheim, thinking solely in a one-dimensional sequence of verbal language is "thoughtless thinking." But thinking by means of a visual medium allows the representation of shapes in both two-dimensional and three-dimensional space. "This polydimensional space not only yields good thought models of physical objects or events, it also represents isomorphically the dimensions needed for theoretical reasoning" (p. 232). The possibilities and limitations of theoretical reasoning in different dimensions will be explored in subsequent chapters. What needs to be stressed here is that neither language nor any other one-dimensional mode is being attacked. The point is that a sign of any dimension must be undergirded by the other dimensions. In addition to the Peircean idea that a linguistic sign refers to a class of things rather than to a concrete object, is the corresponding fact about a visual sign constructed on a two-dimensional plane. For example, Jean

Piaget and Barbara Inhelder have explained that if perception is an understanding of objects by means of direct apprehension, then representation or imagination evoke absent objects and thereby aid in perception.[16] So, "one may recognize a 'triangle' and liken the given figure to the entire class of comparable shapes not present to perception" (p. 17). Long ago, Aristotle speculated about the same figure: "though we do not for the purpose of the proof make use of the fact that the quantity in the triangle (for example, which we have drawn) is determinate, we nevertheless draw it determinate in quantity."[17] All signs, tools, and models of discovery, although determinate in their construction, point to the indeterminate meaning of their class.

For every act of limitation implies a transcendence. In Chapter 4 we shall see how semiotic selection displaces, by suppressing, one set of alternative signs that have not been chosen, while the selection simultaneously fails to delimit a larger set. That indeterminacy is the reason why the semiotic dimension is hypothetical. In this book the boundary conditions by which signs of various dimensions evoke their indeterminate classes will be explained by the figure-ground relationship of Gestalt psychology. For three-dimensional signs both set forth and suppress the ground of their construction, two-dimensional signs similarly evoke the plane, and one-dimensional signs are points extrapolated from time, but which nonetheless evoke sequence.

Sacred Space

Figure-ground semiotics can be used to explore ancient rites of the crane dance, as well as other human rituals, where the figures are dancers and the ground is a literal site. And the hypothetical locus of semiotic discourse can be equated with the "sacred space" set aside by Johan Huizinga for describing the site of transcendent acts of ritual.[18] The crucial element of "play" in sacred performances of early cultures demands that a sacred space be explicitly hedged off in a "temporarily real world of its own" (p. 14). For Huizinga and others, ritual dances re-present acts of nature and so urge nature to keep the world in its right course and to remain benevolent to the dancers. E. A. Armstrong explains that the crane dance was part of a pattern of sacrificial and funerary rites that extended from the Fertile Crescent east and west to China and the Aegean; hence its counterparts are to be discerned in the minotaur's labyrinth and in Chinese underground passages.[19] Dances, in other words, are figures that require a formulaic maze, a substructural ground that evokes the cosmic happening. This classification according to structural and functional similarities allows the conjecture that crane dances are part of a totemic grammar that groups creatures of one leg (birds, animals, or humans) into an order of unipeds which signifies hobbling, lurching, and leaping in the maze. Otherwise diverse creatures can be grouped pedomorphically in this fantastic class: partridge dancers who hold one foot cocked to strike, serpent-tailed daemons of Oriental cultures, Hephaestus and Vulcan who hobbled, Tantalus which means 'lurching', and Oedipus which means 'sore-foot' or perhaps 'one-foot'.[20] The totemic logic would be the hesitational stance of signaling itself, as a bird's teetering on a limb is ritualized into a sign of warning. The emblem of this class of signalers would be the ancient morris-maze pattern of the *triskelés* or swastika which signifies 'fly-foot'.[21] The common structural pattern is an exchange—with displacement that evokes a cosmic order, but in a place and way set aside from the true order.

The rite is a cosmic map, where the symbolic space is different from the real space. Sacred space is another way of expressing the hypothetical dimension of semiotics, where the *Danzenplatz* represents the ground of discourse and the lurching and leaping figures represent the signs. The members of the class must leap for the hypothetical dimension, of Nature. As discontinuous signs of mediation they serve as go-betweens, as shamans that evoke the class. As members they also evoke the class: they draw back to leap higher. This is the knight's gambit in chess: up a square and over two. The process of ritualization therefore includes both the synchronic paradox of member and class plus the diachronic paradox of ontogeny and phylogeny.

Accommodation

These ritual dances enact an ancient rhetorical trope of "accommodation" in which human language, used to evoke the sympathy of the gods, cannot hope to imitate the visionary language of the supernatural order. As John Milton phrased it in *Paradise Lost:*

> what surmounts the reach
> Of human sense, I shall delineate so,
> By lik'ning spiritual to corporeal forms,
> As may express them best, though what if Earth
> Be but the Shadow of Heav'n, and things therein
> Each to other like, more than on Earth is thought?[22]

The ordinary use of accommodation has a use similar to Huxley's ritualization: the "adaptation of a word, expression, or system to something different from its original purpose." But in many archaic cultures, accommodation was not simply a failure of human language or acts, but rather a fear of imitating exactly objects of veneration or awe. The Anglo-Saxon 'kenning' (world-candle for sun, word-hoard for mind, head-jewels for eyes) is but one example of a periphrastic form that took the long way around in order to displace the equivalence betwixt word and thing. For Ortega y Gasset, metaphor originates with this form of taboo.[23] And for Sigmund Freud this form of accommodation defines the distinctive state of human beings. Mankind is a "prosthetic God" who is magnificent when he puts on those auxiliary organs, "but those organs have not grown on to him and they still give him much trouble at times."[24] Furthermore,

> A good part of the struggles of mankind centre around the single task of finding an expedient accommodation—one, that is, that will bring human happiness—between this claim of the individual and the cultural claims of the group; and one of the problems that touches the fate of humanity is whether such an accommodation can be reached by some particular form of civilization or whether this conflict is irreconcilable (p. 43).

Much more prosaic is Lévi-Strauss's "bricoleur," the odd-job man who accommodates himself to a task by using a limited repertoire of means at his disposal for whatever contingency.[25] He explains that the old meaning of the word "bricoleur" referred to "some extraneous movement: a ball rebounding, a dog straying, or a horse swerving from its direct course to avoid an obstacle" (p. 16).

The semiotic meaning of accommodation therefore involves the awareness that any sign, tool, or model evokes a discontinuity when it has been transferred from one category of use to another. As a form of leaping, swerving, or lurching, as a form of accommodation, that is, the sign always evinces torsion. Shakespeare's Timon of Athens once said, "All is oblique." Torsion will be an important term in this study. Semiotic torsion is observed most clearly in things such as Found Art or in fine art such as Picasso's "Baboon with Young," which features a recognizable toy automobile welded onto the torso of a baboon. Torsion is that "push-pull" phenomenon which one experiences as he sees in a painting the semblance of a landscape and then the medium of painted brushstrokes. A sign is like any bounded line that exhibits a torsion between separation and connection, difference and sameness, Snout and his Wall.

When a sign, tool, or model accommodates itself to the task of connecting two categories that were originally separate, it always evinces a torsion that indicates its jointure is not absolutely fitting. Torsion will therefore be used in subsequent chapters as one of the increments in arriving at the six categories of signs. If ritualization defines the diachronic process, if accommodation means an imperfect semiotic fitting, and if torsion defines the observed discontinuity in a sign, then two elementary principles emerge from the construction of any dimensional sign. First, most cultures have celebrated Aristotle's bionic dictum, expressed by Alexander Pope as "First follow Nature." Second, every imitation accommodates some Platonic awareness that the model is a poor imitation, a distortion of the hypothetical dimension, in this case, Nature. These principles may be illustrated by Figures 2 and 3. According to Joseph Needham, the Chinese junk looks strange to Western eyes, because one does not recognize the natural origin of its design.[26] Junks were modeled after the

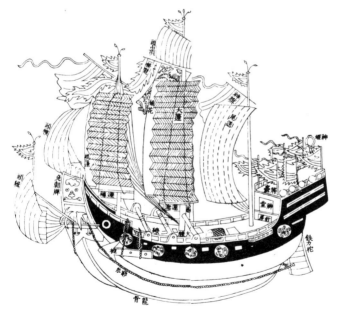

FIG. 2. In the design of this Chinese ocean-going junk one can discern a water bird as its bionic model. From *Liu-Chhiu Chih Lüeh* (1757). Harvard Yenching Library.

FIG. 3. In this technical drawing of a sixteenth-century hull one can see a submerged fish as its bionic model. From the Matthew Baker manuscript in the Pepysian Library. By permission of the Master and Fellows, Magdalene College, Cambridge.

order palmipeds, webbed-footed birds such as pelicans, petrels, and swans, whose buoyancy is buffeted both by water and by air. Most of the outlandishness disappears as one observes the high tail, the bluff breast, the eyes, and the face, indeed, the seaworthiness of a water bird hidden in the outline. The other illustration is an Elizabethan shipwright's, Matthew Baker, who superimposed a fish upon the hull in order to visualize the designer's maxim: "a cod's head and a mackerel's tail." Two different kinds of animal helped determine shape, but one was airborne, and the other was submerged.

Ships are particularly vivid examples for introducing principles of accommodation, because they are radicals of semiotic transfer. As a transporting vehicle, a ship exchanges information from a source to a recipient, and vice versa, by traversing two dissimilar media, the land and the sea. As a sign it seems to be autonomous, independent upon the sea, while really remaining dependent upon its surrounding contexts, its ports. The ancient cult of the ship springs from this seemingly magical independence. The most familiar personification of this cult is the daemon Charon the Porter. In the theory of logical types a ship as container is superior to its contents, but the periphrasis of synecdoche, of substituting the container for the thing contained, was useful when a ship was ritualized from utilitarian needs to funerary rites.[27] The pattern is one of exchange-with-displacement, wherein the ship's bionic origin combines with its supernatural end to transport stuffs from this world to another.

The Grecian cult of the independent ship was responsible for the beginnings of scientific discovery, according to Ortega y Gasset:

> . . . when the Greeks set themselves to dreaming, they would dream of ships, capable in themselves, withc it a pilot, of bringing the sailor safe to port. These are the mysterious ships of the Phoenicians, and when one begins to study them, there on the coast of Ionia, in Miletus, a society of men emerges presided over by Thales, which calls itself The Forever Sailors (Siempre Navigantes); these celebrate their scientific sessions in a boat on the high seas. And thus, in one way or another, the idea of the ship enters into the most profound and moving depths of the ancient soul. Hence its cult of the ship and of opportunity, for *opportunitus* means nothing more or less than the way which leads us to the *portus*, or port.[28]

According to Herodotus, Thales was a merchant of Phoenician extraction; it is therefore logical that the first Greek model of scientific discovery depended upon a ship's semiotic qualities. For Thales wrote, "the earth is supported by water on which it rides like a ship."[29] And for George Thomson, Thales' adage was in keeping with an even older idea, of "the waters that are beneath the earth," the Babylonian *apsu*.[30] As a ship is to water, so earth is to the *apeiron*: the semiotic figure, limited in itself, accommodates an indeterminate ground by imitation and distortion. In this book, therefore, accommodation is to be construed as a general term for a series of transformations that result in a semiotic complex of display and displacement. In a later section the transformations will be divided into three operations, where the dimensional aspects of any sign are (1) Highlighted, (2) Torqued, (3) Suppressed.

Means-Ends Conversions

The cause of the origin of a thing and its eventual utility, its actual employment and place in a system of purpose, lie worlds apart; whatever exists, having somehow come into being, is again and again reinterpreted to new ends, taken over, transformed, redirected by some power superior to it; all events in the organic world are a subduing, a *becoming master*, and all subduing and becoming master involves a fresh interpretation, and adaptation through which any previous 'meaning' and 'purpose' are necessarily obscured or obliterated.

Nietzsche,
On the Genealogy of Morals

Our inventions are wont to be pretty toys, which distract our attention from serious things. They are but improved means to an unimproved end, an end which was already but too easy to arrive at—as railroads lead to Boston or New York. We are in great haste to construct a magnetic telegraph from Maine to Texas; but Maine and Texas, it may be, have nothing to communicate.

Thoreau, *Walden*

Acts that were primitively spontaneous are converted into means that make human intercourse more rich and gracious—just as a painter converts pigment into means for expressing an imaginative experience.

Dewey, *Art as Experience*

It is precisely this 'metaphorical transference' which contains our whole problem in a nutshell.

Cassirer, *Essay on Man*

    A useful way to define the terms 'sign', 'tool', and 'model' is by way of means-ends analysis. As the epigraphs attest, a conversion from means to ends is a variant of semiotic exchange and displacement. One agrees with Nietzsche that it is difficult to discern, for example, the neolithic origins of clay in finished pottery, or of copper powder in elegant bronze, or of flax in linen, or indeed of grapes in wine. On the other hand, Thoreau has his followers who claim that means have been ritualized into unnatural prominence so that, for example, industrialization exaggerates a necessary mode of maintaining social goods into an overriding end, just as the Prussian state made a fetish of militarism.[31] The ethics of "ought" is part of a philosophical corrective to instrumentalism that must be understood.[32] Yet the more neutral task of defining the categories of transference and their observed torsion will take precedence here.

For John Dewey, a sign occurs as an "expressed" need, and it is converted from the very materials that seem to block immediate action. "Etymologically, an act of expression is a squeezing out, a pressing forth. Juice is expressed when grapes are crushed in the wine press . . . ."[33] The deflection of raw material into a medium or expression converts obstacles into means or media by way of thinking or of "reflection." The formal cause of pressure, coming both from without, in the environment, and from within the body, converts the blockage into a sign, a Matterhorn.

It is possible to lay signs, tools, and models in a sliding scale of means and ends. Charles Morris said that "something is a sign only because it is interpreted as a sign of something by some interpreter. . . . Semiotics, then, is not concerned with the study of a particular kind of object, but only with ordinary objects insofar (and only insofar) as they participate in semiosis."[34] Hence, a sign is construed here to be anything that has been ritualized from one category of use toward a new end so that it is seen by an interpreter as accommodating the place of something else. Although the definition usefully includes the several terms so far isolated—ritualization, accommodation, and torsion—it does not yet discriminate among the different functions of signs, tools, and models. Now let us follow one example in order to define signs, tools, and models in terms of means-end conversions.

To Hamlet the skull of Yorick is a *memento mori*, a sign to him about existence. But a skull as a three-dimensional sign need not necessarily betoken the futility of earthly pleasures. Consider the way that Goethe "turned" a skull to his own ends. Helmholtz mentions this anecdote about discovery in "Goethe's Scientific Researches": "A fortunate glance at a broken sheep's skull, which Goethe found by accident on the sand of the Lido at Venice, suggested to him that the skull itself consisted of a series of very much altered vertabrae."[35] Devoid of intentionality, the skull was insightfully interpreted as being in itself a fused symptom of physiological development. Goethe saw the torsion in the sign by decomposing it and then reconstructing it on a different plane of signification. Or consider the skull that Pericles found, and its subsequent use as a prophetic sign of subsequent events. Plutarch tells how one day the popular leader brought from his farm to Athens a ram's head that had only one horn. A diviner told Pericles that the single horn growing strangely out of the skull was sign or token of fate, indicating that of the two factions in the city, his and that of Thucydides, the leadership of Athens would eventually devolve upon the owner of the farm where the sheep was found. Anaxagoras, however, took to the tools of natural philosophy, dissected the skull, and gave a physiological explanation for the distorted growth of a single horn. For this answer he was much admired, until Pericles subsequently came to power. Plutarch's summary is so clearly honed as to be a parable about an ancient linguistic theory:

> And yet, in my opinion, it is no absurdity to say that they were both in the right, both natural philosopher and diviner, one justly detecting the cause of this event, by which it was produced, the other the end for which it was designed. For it was the business of the one to find out and give an account of what it was made, and in what manner and by what means it grew as it did; and of the other to foretell to what end and purpose it was so made, and what it might mean or portend. Those who say that to find out the cause of a prodigy is in effect to destroy its supposed significance as such, do not take notice, that, at the same time, together with divine prodigies, they also do away with signs and signals of human art and

concert, as, for instance, the clashing of quoits, fire-beacons, and the shadows of sun-dials, every one of which has its cause, and by that cause and contrivance is a sign of something else.[36]

This passage drives a wedge into the question of antecedents and consequents with which we opened the chapter. As we shall see in Chapter 4, the structural question "Where did the skull come from?" is logically different from the prophetic question, "What is it for?" But to question the form and function of signs is to make of them an illogical composite. All three examples verify our starting point, that signs are limited objects which are enjoined to stand for something else; meaning stands apart from their original composition, as the means vary from the ends.

However, unless we limit our definition to hand-held tools, the examples serve also to define tools at large. Although a tool might be considered to be any object "turned" to a new kind of manual operation, the definition should include instruments of more distant extension that are still under control of human hands. For instance, one of the first tools was a "dawn stone," with a rudimentary percussed edge, but the class of cutting tools should include such distal instruments as plow, keel, stylus, intaglio cylinder—all probes which figuratively describe furrows of significance upon their grounds. Beginning as hand-held and dependent upon the kinesthesia of body movement, tools become more and more distant from manual labor as they are applied more widely to different ends. By extending the definition, however, one has overlapped into the category of models. Although skulls could be placed with the class of container tools, they were interpreted as three models for the way the world performs. So let us define models as tools whose utility has been extended and so transformed that they are no longer means to a different end but are mirrors of the problematic end itself. For, the increasing application of an effective tool to wider areas of endeavor renders it a model by reason of its near universality: the principle of the Egyptian astronomer's *gnomon* gradually becomes transformed into the cosmic law of the Great Pyramid; the rope knotted lengthwise into ratios of 3–4–5, used as measuring tools by Mesopotamian surveyors, becomes a Pythagorean model for the chord music of the spheres; a device such as a watch becomes a model for a mechanistic universe. Each of these examples will be discussed in subsequent chapters.

In other words, the wider application of an exosomatic instrument to the world implies that the laws which had governed the working of a tool have become so useful at large that, by synecdoche, they come to substitute for the world. When a tool is 'turned' from its intended use and contemplated instead of applied, the arbitrary connection between a tool and its referred function is transformed so that it is no longer a means to a different end. Seen as reflections of the end itself, the principles by which a tool are constructed may be construed as hieroglyphs, omens, signatures, symptoms, laws, or models of higher function. Our definitions therefore are perspectivist; depending upon the oblique perspective given a semiotic object, it becomes sign, tool, or model.

To recapitulate, a model functions as a simpler substitute for a problem less easily understood: "No substantial part of the universe is so simple that it can be grasped and controlled without abstraction. Abstraction consists in replacing the part of the universe under consideration by a model of similar but simpler structure."[37] A model tends to reflect an end state, while ignoring the means to a different end. This complex accords with Herbert A. Snow's description of means-ends analysis.[38] For him all problem solving is divided among process descriptions and state descriptions, means and ends, recipes and blueprints: "To construct a circle, rotate a compass with one arm fixed until the other arm has reached its starting point. . . . A circle is the locus of all points equidistant from a given point" (p. 479). All organisms survive by combining the two, which we verbalize as means-ends analysis: "Given a desired state of affairs and an existing state of affairs, the task of an adaptive organism is to find the difference between these two states, and then to find the correlative process that will find the difference" (p. 479). One imagines a blueprint of the future state and then seeks out a recipe as a means. Because spatio-temporal axes are intertwined here, we shall diagram, in the next section, the several dimensional possibilities of signs. Then these six possibilities of semiotic discourse can display different torsions of means and ends.

Semiotic Dimensions

One of the far-reaching issues which confronts the several disciplines of science and the humanities is a distortion that can result from the transfer of a successful discovery from one of those disciplines to serve a need in a field for which the new method was not originally designed. In the history of ideas, for example, the successes of Newtonian mechanics, of Darwinian evolution, of information theory, might be gauged by their widespread misapplication in remote disciplines. The complete substitution of the model for a different problem produced cross-categorical sports such as the interiorization of Newtonian space inside the head of Lockean psychology, the transformation of natural selection into an economic principle justifying Herbert Spencer's dog-eat-dog theories, and the chess-playing computer that would subjugate man. I do not intend to demean the cross-categorical method. On the contrary, it is clear that in many cases the transfers have been intellectually enlightening or socially effective. Think of William Harvey's application of a hydraulic principle to the heart's circulation of blood, or of the ethologists' redirection of natural selection toward a better understanding of territory, or of geneticists' and physiologists' transfers of information theory to their disciplines. In the examples where distortions have occurred, methods were thought of as universal panaceas; where they were effective, revolutionary models were understood to be special cases of wider phenomena which the original designers had not imagined. The study of models in itself is a special case of a semiotic study that highlights the limits both of remaining within strict categories and of transcending them.

As the study of signs regardless of particular disciplines, semiotics allows the arrangement of symbolic discourse into a new category of Euclidean dimensions, one that classifies instruments according to their use in space. Because semiotics does not limit itself to the science of linguistic signs, but includes signs outside of language within its purview, models of scientific discovery therefore can be considered as a special case of the more inclusive question of the dimensional locus of man's artificial extensions. Let us begin by comparing models with linguistic signs and hand-held tools. By exercising variations upon a pioneering diagram of semiotics drawn by C. S. Peirce, we can better understand the hypothetical dimension of symbolic discourse, no matter whether it be a hammer that exists in three dimensions, a pictographic model on a two-dimensional plane, or a one-dimensional linguistic sign (Figure 4).

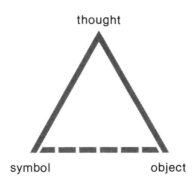

FIG. 4. An often-used semiotic triangle designed to show an imputed relation between symbol and referent.

In *The Meaning of Meaning* Ogden and Richards appropriated this diagram in order to stress the indirect relation that exists between a symbol or verbal expression and the object or referent which is referred to.[39] And Umberto Eco provides an excellent analysis of a possible "referential fallacy" in the diagram, which he reveals by comparing Ogden and Richards' diagram with a similar construction of C. S. Peirce's and one of Frege's.[40] For Ogden and Richards most of the misunderstanding that language transposes to physics or philosophy arises from the indirect relation between symbol and referent, or signifier and signified. "Every great advance in physics has been at the expense of some generally accepted piece of metaphysical explanation which has enshrined itself in a convenient, universally practised, symbolic shorthand" (p. 14). The diagram serves as a specific reminder that thought, directed by knowledge of the conventions of language, yokes the dissimilarities into unity. Since for Ogden and Richards language is a "ready instrument," the handy telescoping along the dotted line is more important than the relative inaccuracy of neglecting to include the interpreter's thought processes: "Thus such a shorthand as the word 'means' is constantly used to imply a direct simple relation between words and things, phrases and situations" (p. 14). It is precisely that neglect of the mental process which causes many unnecessarily inaccurate intrusions of semiotic conventions upon the satisfactory solution of a problem.

In Figure 5 we can stress the dimensional aspects of the linguistic sign by locating at B the signifier as a pictorial expression that exists on a two-dimensional plane when written. If the linguistic sign that we are examining is the word "piston," we shall enclose it with two slashes //piston// in order to isolate the two-dimensional visual image of the signifier. Similarly, let C represent the signified three-dimensional object, whose physical properties can be referred to as ///piston///. For Ogden and Richards, it was thinking along the relational axes, here depicted

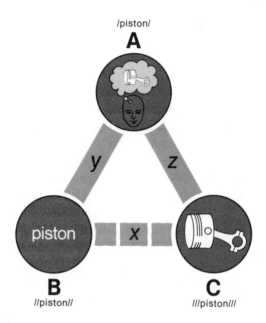

FIG. 5. Diagram depicting the semiotic relation between the written word "piston" and its imputed object. The slashes number the pertinent dimension.

as y and z, that unified the linguistic triangle at A. Since mentation is here considered a process rather than a thing, let A represent the one-dimensional relation that temporally processes the linguistic sign along y and z. When we wish to highlight the thought process that allows the handy shortcut from B to C, we shall refer to the process as /piston/, which thus reveals its nonexistence in space and thereby provides a reason for the indirect relation along x. For thought seems unneeded, not being seen, in the seemingly direct relation existing between thought and thing.

Let us initially propose that linguistic signs exist primarily in a one-dimensional mode, since in the time that they are being used one reads from the two-dimensional signifier to the three-dimensional object. Reasons for this designation will be presented further on, and in Chapter 3 at large. Consider that even though all signs are in time, many are not linguistic, but some are two-dimensional pictographs, such as international road signs, or three-dimensional, such as Hamlet's reading of Yorick's skull.

For purposes of comparison, consider in Figure 6 how tool usage can be adapted to the semiotic triangle. In performing a utilitarian task such as hammering, one again assumes the indirect relationship between symbol and object, that //hammer//, means ///hammer///. Hence, draw once again the dotted line along x as a reminder of the arbitrary shortcut that is taken. But consider that while one is hammering, no direct relation is made

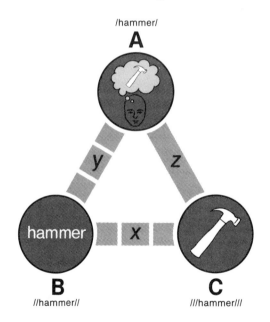

Fig. 6. Diagram depicting the act of hammering, in which no relation exists with the visual image of the written word //hammer//.

with the pictorial images of the word //hammer//. While I am driving a nail, I do not think, "Hammer, hammer, hammer!" Hence y is similarly dotted in order to suggest the subsidiary state of that axis in tool usage. It might be argued that z is also arbitrary, since the relation between a ///hammer/// and its employment is not limited to the designed structure of the object. A hammer may be misappropriated for an indefinite number of tasks other than that of driving nails. However, for the purposes of the semiotic triangle the present issue is not the different ends for which an instrument such as a hammer might be employed. Rather, the point here is that in the act of hammering anything a direct relation exists with A and C along z as thought impels the object, as /hammer/ wields the ///hammer///. Before evaluating the differences between linguistic signs and tools, one must realign the semiotic diagram in order to observe its fittingness for accommodating a model of discovery.

One difference between models and either linguistic signs or tools is crucial to discern. We have construed a linguistic sign to be a one-dimensional set of two-dimensional signifiers connected with three-dimensional objects by virtue of an arbitrary and indirect convention that we have sketched as a dotted line along x. We have stated that a tool also maintains the indirect link at x, and although it has not been depicted in Figure 6 above, we stipulated that the relation between ///hammer/// and purpose is arbitrary. But a model of discovery functions as a simpler hypothetical substitute for a problem less easily understood. That is, a linguistic sign links *arbitraries* together by a remembered convention, while a model predicts *similarities* between itself and a problem that is too complex to grasp in its totality. A model, furthermore, is a link between a theory and experiment. When we construct a dimensional reduction that models a joint or a synapse, for instance, we are examining a connecting principle, a "link" that has evolved in the spatio-temporal enterprise as a model of that enterprise.

In order to make the comparison of the diagrams more symmetrical, let us continue to use a three-dimensional object for modeling, as we have with ///piston/// and ///hammer///, although we recall that models, like signs and tools, may be designed to work in other dimensions, such as two-dimensional blueprints or one-dimensional chemical equations. A serviceable model with which to display and displace a universe is a ///sphere///. The semiotic triangle in Figure 7 must be modified so that the arbitrary linkage at x is retained, where there is no inherent similarity between //sphere// at B and ///sphere/// at C that substitutes for a universe. Since, however, the ///sphere/// incorporates or will incorporate features that characterize the universe to be comprehended, we should depict an

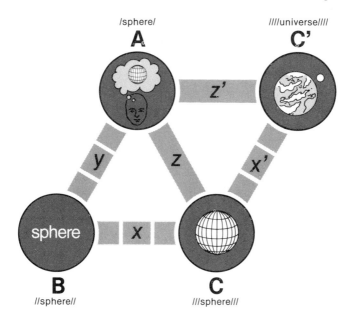

Fɪɢ. 7. Diagram depicting the use of a 3D model, such as a sphere, to substitute for a problem of partially understood properties at C'.

axis of thought that would show the relationship of similarity, if not identity, between model and problem. If we construct C' to represent the tacit end of the problem, in an n-dimensional problematic universe, that displacement into an explicitly hypothetical dimension would more graphically depict the displacement that has taken place once we substitute a simpler model for a more complicated problem. In drawing the tangent x' from the model at C to the projected and unknown end at C', we mean that one solves the indirect relation at x' by thinking along z and z'.

The discussion has focused so far upon the differences and similarities shared by tools, signs, and models in a semiotic triangle which was arranged so that the three different kinds of exosomatic instruments had a common three-dimensional point at C. That means one can interchange the examples in Figures 5, 6, and 7. Pistons and spheres are used as tools, while as cranks and discs they once served as parts of La Mettrie's model of a human machine. And of course the diagrams are meant to remind us that each of the objects has a linguistic signifier which is arbitrarily attached. By showing that three-dimensional objects may be freely interchanged in the several semiotic triangles, have we slurred distinctive differences among signs, tools, and models? On the contrary, by emphasizing the dimensionality of signs, tools, and models, we shall see that traditional definitions in actuality make distinctions where there is no difference.

Now let us vary the semiotic triangle in order to highlight signs, tools, and models that work from a two-dimensional plane. (The diagrams that have been sketched of the semiotic triangle are, of course, two-dimensional examples.) Consider that in Figure 8 we have substituted a two-dimensional pictograph for the three-dimensional model of Figure 7; that is, for an example of a two-dimensional model we have replaced the sphere with a projectional map. In Figure 8, therefore, point C has been deleted from consideration, for we are no longer solving along x', from a three-dimensional model at C to a hypothetical dimension

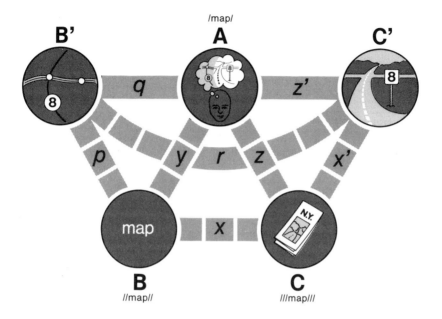

Fig. 8. Diagram depicting the use of a 2D model, such as a road map.

at C'. Neither are we preoccupied with the pictorial images, the signifiers which constitute the figures of a linguistic sign for the word "map" at point B. Hence y and p are axes of suppressed interest in Figure 8 (y representing mentation about the letters and p representing the axes of indirect relation) because connection between signifiers of //map// and the projected blueprint of a universe is capricious. Our concern is with the assumed similarities along r. In other words, thought is focused along q and z' to yield the indirect relationship at r between two-dimensional model and tacit end of the problem, or Δ AB'C'.

If in Figure 8 one wished to consider "map" as a linguistic sign, he could then work with Δ ABC. Similarly, if he wanted to understand the related dimensions of a map as a two-dimensional tool such as a blueprint, he could consider $\triangle$ AB'C. But notice that as a two-dimensional pictographic sign, as distinguished from the linguistic sign at $\triangle$ ABC, the maplike features of the plane are not distinguishable from a two-dimensional tool at $\triangle$ AB'C. If the features of a two-dimensional sign and a two-dimensional tool are congruent, we have simplified our problem in defining them. As a final consideration of Figure 8 we must observe that this triangle does not explain the reasons for the choice of a two-dimensional model and the corresponding displacement of three-dimensional considerations. For instance, Helmholtz once asked a popular audience to play a figure-ground game, to imagine a country of flatlanders who were limited to a two-dimensional plane so that the audience could better understand its experiential limits of being forced to exist in a Euclidean frame of three dimensions. This convenient combination of display and displacement, of observed distortion, will be considered in Figure 10 and in Chapter 2.

Now consider a diagram of one-dimensional signs, tools, and models. We allowed earlier that a linguistic sign is primarily one-dimensional, even though its pictorial images lie on a two-dimensional plane, and, as images, might lie in a heavy book composed of a certain amount of ink and might refer to a three-dimensional object, ///piston///. In the act of reading, however, the pictorial and kinesthetic dimensions are subsumed into the movement of mentation, a process which cannot be described except retrospectively in spatial terminology. Let us describe in Figure 9 a tangent from point A to point C' that represents the thinking process of memory and prediction which comprises the method of reading toward the analytic point of any passage of linguistic signs. The axis z' therefore 'means' that searching toward a hypothetical dimension which characterized z' in Figures 7 and 8. All are one-dimensional probes of a thinking process that moves back and forth from model to hypothesis. Is there

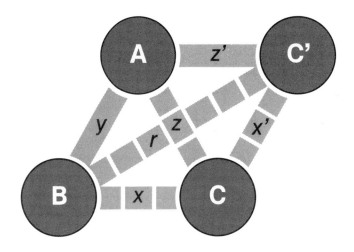

Fɪɢ. 9. Diagram illustrating the act of reading, from linguistic sign to imputed meaning.

then a difference between a linguistic sign and a one-dimensional tool or model? As soon as a one-dimensional sign is set to work by thought, it is indistinguishable from anything else we might call a one-dimensional tool or model. For we are discussing that category of semiotic exchanges that includes any series of notations, whether it be a mathematical equation for a chemical process, a score in music, or a passage from *Oliver Twist*; all refer to the same kind of hypothetical point of attention at C', reached by remembering and predicting along z'. Thus all three instruments have features which are congruent along Δ ABC' in Figure 9.

Notice that one is unable to depict a point at A', which would represent pure process, for images pictured in some kind of space are required in any one-dimensional construct. In Chapter 3 a one-dimensional sign will be studied as a semiotic *point* of reference extrapolated from specific instances in time. Hence it is technically zero-dimensional in a Euclidean sense. So Figure 9 allows the visualization of that process at point A. As we recall from Figure 5, B represents the two-dimensional aspects of the linguistic sign, or tool, or model. As signifier, it is decoded from a conventional memory bank in order to probe C'. Just as in Figure 1 the axis x was construed to be an indirect relation between signifier and signified, so in Figure 9 the axis r "means" an indirect relation between signifier and tacit problem. What does it mean that one-dimensional signs, tools, and models are congruent at Δ ABC'? It has the same significance as the observation that two-dimensional signs and tools are congruent along Δ AB'C' in Figure 8. The verbal distinctions between the three kinds, as well as their dictionary definitions, are meaningless in operation.

One-dimensional probing along the axis of z' may be characterized by the relational unit $(n+1)$. If random mentation and random history may be considered as a succession of discrete events without semblance of causation, mathematics and history seem to have begun with the desire to extrapolate an orderly sense of twoness separate from specific objects or events in time. History and mathematics may be said to begin intuitively with the desire to transcend time. The relational sequence $(n+1)$ is therefore a serviceable mnemonic for representing the mentation process along the vertical axes of the depicted triangles. Thinking along an arithmetical continuum of $(n+1)$, where there is no finite analytical boundary and where there is no temporal limitation, is a serviceable way to describe the orderly accretion of evidence that builds to the hypothetically indefinite end for which signs, tools, and models substitute.

Similarly, the lines of indirect relation that we have drawn as dotted lines at the bases of the triangles may be described as a unit of $(n-1)$. We use the relation $(n-1)$ because the bases of the Δ ABC represent a conventional Euclidean sequence in which point, line, plane, and sphere are defined by twisting neighbors ninety degrees. Turning a line at right angles to itself reveals a point; rotating a plane yields a line; a sphere unveils a plane.

Martin Gardner says, "In every space of n dimensions the 'mirror' is a surface of n-1 dimensions."[41] Each point in the original Δ ABC progresses from a lesser to a greater geometrical dimension, so each axis could be represented as turning out of itself by an increment of one twist. By increasingly indirect reversals, one works toward the tacit end of the problem at C' which is 'mirrored' by a model of fewer dimensions.

By combining the two dissimilar categories—the mathematical thought that is extrapolated from time $(n+1)$ plus the geometrical progression of $(n-1)$—we seem to leap from point A to point C' by $(n\pm1)$. This combination is useful to realize because $(n+1)$ reminds us that mentation is self-consciously included in discovery, while $(n-1)$ implies that the mirror of mind has been deleted. Following Ogden and Richards, we infer that on the one hand mentation seems outside the semiotic bases of geometrical relation, yet on the other hand we know that mentation makes the connections. So the combination $(n\pm1)$ means a complex dialectic between model and tacit problem via a mentation process that is both within and without the modular system being described. From the outside we see the model as an object with geometrical qualities; seen from within, the model is processional, that is, arithmetical. That twofold perspective prompts most of the problems about "meta" languages, but we must ignore them for the more pressing task of definition.

Any instrument, whether tool, sign, or model, may be said to manifest obliquity or torsion, since it serves as a dialectical interchange between an object of Euclidean dimensions and a hypothetical problem. The dialectic occurs diagrammatically as thought probes along the vertical axes of our triangles and exchanges characteristics with the basal points so that B 'means' C. We have observed, however, that the exchange is not exact but in all cases indirect. For the features of one dimension have been suppressed and displaced in order to display qualities in another dimension. This functional obliquity, this dialectical system of exchange and displacement, must be examined with some care, for its torquing quality is the very medium of sleight of hand, of deception, and it bears on the potential illusoriness of model building. Consider that the most ancient recorded lie in Western literature is Odysseus' to Polyphemus. Captured by the Cyclops and then asked his name, Odysseus answered with winged words, "Nobody." So when Polyphemus was blinded by the wily mariner and shouted to his neighbors for help, "Nobody is killing me by force or treachery," then Odysseus and his crew escaped to their ship. This diversionary pun draws attention to the ordinarily tacit displacement of the signifier by the signified. The pun probably is as old as the consciousness that a linguistic sign could serve not only to represent a concrete object, as in proto-writing, but could also refer to an abstract concept, as an ideograph. "Nobody" exists 'in' the same hypothetical dimension with Pegasus, with the square circle, with any thought experiment; all are possibilities which are pointed to by signs, tools, or models of a lesser dimension.

Polydimensional Semiotics

Given the functional relativism that governs semiotic definitions, it becomes necessary to reorient the classes of objects according to torsion. For we can now use what we have learned about the apparent torque from one dimension to another in order to isolate the exact number of semiotic objects possible in Euclidean space. In this context there are only six possible ways to represent semiotic objects; that small number offsets the relativism of indefinite possibilities of use. In Figure 10 we have constructed a diagram that depicts the several dimensions of an object as if they were seen simultaneously from different perspectives.

The nearest position on any axis depicts the dominant dimension of a semiotic object; that view highlights the dimension

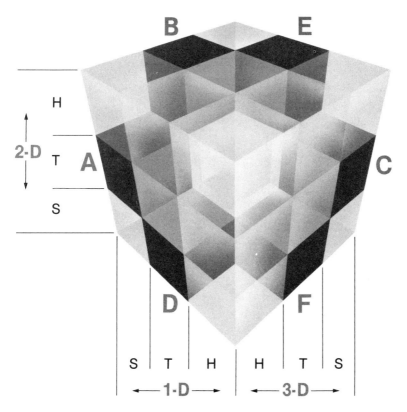

Fɪɢ. 10. A modified Guilford cube that shows the six dimensions categorized in this book. To decipher their components, follow the implicit axes of *x, y,* and *z*. Category A, for instance, represents that category of instruments whose dimensionality features three dimensionality (3D) highlighted (H), two dimensionality (2D) torqued (T), and one dimensionality (1D) suppressed (S).

of primary importance. For example, a neolithic pot exists primarily as a three-dimensional object. The right-hand view suggests the relational axis that is torqued from one dimension to another. To continue the example of the neolithic pot, it is obvious that the pot wall curves away from a two-dimensional plane toward containment. But the two-dimensional plane upon which designs of any kind are executed tends to be dematerialized as does the three-dimensional pot itself, when one reads the meaning of the described figures on it. Or consider that a highly symmetrical flaking on a flint knife turns attention away from function toward the elegance of two-dimensional patterning. This perspectivist twist of attention back and forth from function to pattern will demand discussion further on. All of the sides furthest from the viewer are meant to suggest the dimension that is suppressed in a semiotic object. For instance, the one-dimensional aspect of a neolithic pot is suppressed, even though in making it the pot's symmetry depended upon a spinning potting wheel or the regular movement of skilled hands. Let the furthest extreme of the box diagram, which also cannot be depicted, be the assumed horizon of a sign, tool, or model; that is, let that extreme side represent the semiotic function of an instrument, the hypothetical dimension which it probes at C'. The conceptual horizon of a neolithic pot is indefinite: it means holding grain; it means the ceremony of the harvest as well as the ritual of the grave; it means Ingres' *La Source,* or the water pot of the woman of Samaria. Its allusive powers are limited only by the constraints of imagination. We can therefore plot A as the class of three-dimensional objects such as pots and knives which torque two-dimensionality and suppress one-dimensionality.

Let B represent all instruments which are primarily two-dimensional, such as the cave paintings of Lascaux, or Egyptian hieroglyphs, or international road signs, in other words, that class which exists primarily on a two-dimensional plane, which torques three-dimensionality and suppresses one-dimensionality. On all such planes the illusion of depth is achieved by the familiar torsion of the figure slanted so as to achieve seeming independence from ground. The image is obviously static; one-dimensionality cannot be expressed pictorially. We will later discuss the semblance of movement in certain two-dimensional art forms, but for now we are considering utilitarian semiotic objects, not fine art.

Let C represent the one-dimensional class of instruments, such as abstract notches on primitive tally sticks, or a letter from the phonetic alpahabet where A stands for a sound, or an Arabic numeral such as 2, or a musical notation for C#. In this class a point arrested from time is highlighted, with two-dimensionality torqued as one turns from the pictorial image to its meaning, while the three-dimensional aspects, the material components such as the iota of ink that comprises the figure and the elements of paper that comprise the ground, are suppressed.

Given the combination of 3–2–1 dimensions, and given the three variations of "highlight," "torque," and "suppress," there are merely a total of six possible combinations that complete the class of semiotic instruments:

A - 3D highlighted - 2D torqued - 1D suppressed
B - 2D highlighted - 3D torqued - 1D suppressed
C - 1D highlighted - 2D torqued - 3D suppressed
D - 3D highlighted - 1D torqued - 2D suppressed
E - 2D highlighted - 1D torqued - 3D suppressed
F - 1D highlighted - 3D torqued - 2D suppressed

What kinds of semiotic objects might satisfy the remaining combinations of D, E, F?

Examples will be more readily forthcoming once we consider that this exercise is derived from Galileo's classification by rank of the several kinds of art forms. Erwin Panofsky reports that in a letter to an artist friend, Galileo had argued that painting, not sculpture, should be ranked more highly. One passage is worth presenting in its entirety, because Galileo's ranking of art forms according to their dimensionality will not only provide us with examples for the remaining possibilities, but also will help explain the relationship of art forms to utilitarian semiotic objects.

> ... the farther removed the means by which one imitates are from the thing to be imitated, the more worthy of wonder the imitation will be. In ancient times those actors who could tell a whole story exclusively by means of movements and gestures were more highly appreciated than those who expressed it *viva voce* in tragedy or comedy, because the former used a means very different and a mode of representation quite divergent from the actions represented. Will we not admire a musician who moves us to sympathy with a lover by representing his sorrows and passions in a song much more than if he were to do it by sobs? And this we do because a song is a medium not only different from but opposite to the [natural] expression of pain while tears and sobs are very similar to it. And we would admire him much more if he were to do it silently, with an instrument only, by means of dissonances and passionate musical accents, for the inanimate strings are [of themselves] less capable of awakening the hidden passions of our soul than is the voice that narrates them. For this reason, then, what will be so wonderful in imitating "sculptress nature" by sculpture itself, in representing that which is relieved by relief itself? Certainly nothing or very little, and the most artistic imitation will be that which represents relief on its opposite, which is the plane. In this respect, therefore, painting is more wonderful than sculpture.[42]

Of course, the means-ends argument really suggests that wordless music is most wonderful among the several arts, because it imitates by the most indirect means. In other words, music, as we noted earlier, belongs to that class of one-dimensional models which imitate the hypothetical dimension with little recourse to the two-dimensional plane and the three-dimensional object.

In accord with Galileo's line of thought let us test music as an example of class F, where the one-dimensionality of movement and tempo is highlighted, with the three-dimensional axis torqued into the apparent shape of harmonic structure, and the two-dimensional plane suppressed. It is three-dimensional obliqueness in one-dimensional art forms that allows literary and music critics to speak of those processional modes in static terms of structure. Correspondingly, the semblance of one-dimensionality in painting allows art critics to speak of apparent motion therein. Music differs from the musical note in class C as the means differ from the end. Similarly, painting as a fine art inhabits class E. Its one-dimensional torque, that provides the semblance of movement in a static representation of nature, differs from a utilitarian pictograph of two dimensions as music differs from musical notation. A stylized representation of a bison at Lascaux, for instance, is a partial sign of a larger meaning derived from the whole composition of bison, deer, and other animal signs on the wall; the composition refers to a hypothetical dimension whose meaning we do not know exactly but which has to do with the paleolithic cult of the hunt. Other art forms, such as mime or ballet, provide examples that fit the three-dimensional requirements of class D. As William Butler Yeats said in "Among School Children":

> O body swayed to music, O brightening glance,
> How can we know the dancer from the dance?

The diagram helps to explain the relation of utilitarian semiotic objects to fine art. If $\frac{A}{D}$ as $\frac{B}{E}$ as $\frac{C}{F}$, then the different ways in which objects are torqued determine their category. The neolithic pot which was placed in class A becomes a sample of fine art in D as the potter incorporates the semblance of one-dimensional movement into the pot. He provides it with delicate S-shaped curvature, makes its walls extremely thin, incorporates swirling lines on the plane; it seems to defy gravity; it dances.

Galileo's definition of art is in the classical tradition of *imitatio* that began with Aristotle. Art imitates nature. His further stipulation, that music and painting imitate by dimensions opposite to their original, accords with our definition of model building. Models used in scientific discovery are simpler dimensional reflections or imitations of a hypothetical dimension that is probed by an object of dimensions different from the point at C'. As imitations, therefore, rather than utilitarian tools which are means to a different end, models seem to fit with imitative art forms in classes D, E, F.

But how can that be so? The significance of the divergent grouping occurs when one separates semiotic objects, as we have seen, according to arbitrary but handy axes of relation on the one hand, or to axes of relative similitude on the other. In the first group consisting of A, B, C, one thinks 'through' the object to a different conceptual horizon 'in' a hypothetical dimension. That is, in all cases the object is interpreted as standing in the place of something else. A code is required for thought to process the relation from //piston// to ///piston///. But as we noticed before, the one-dimensional coding process of mentation is suppressed. The coding seems extrinsic to the handy yoking along x, where //piston// means ///piston///. In class A and B one-dimensionality is suppressed; in class C, though it is highlighted, one looks through it, as a point extrapolated from movement, to its referred meaning. But in the classes that include fine arts and models we note that a semblance of one-dimensionality is represented in the object. That is, in classes D, E, F, the coding process of mentation $(n+1)$ is torqued into the object so that it seems self-referring, understandable on its own terms. As Galileo observed, the wonder of fine art depends upon an awareness of divergent means in the construction. We see both the imitation and the limitation imposed by a different medium. The same twofold awareness occurs in model building, except that we do not simply admire the handiwork, but we always recall the built-in code which displaces at the same time that it imitates the hypothetical problem. It incorporates both $(n+1)$ and $(n-1)$, the twofold perspective of knowing within and without.

We have seen that according to Figure 10 there is a dimensional grammar of six possible semiotic representations of objects. All six variables are limited to the conventional world of three space, but all point to a hypothetical dimension which includes an indefinite number of possible problems beyond Euclid. Semiotics, therefore, can be a useful method for instructing students in the basic structure and function of the professional implements to which they will choose to apprentice themselves. Although semiotics cannot substitute for the professional training of working practically with signs, tools, and models in a particular discipline, it can help to delineate the possibilities and pitfalls of symbolic discourse, an activity which is central to a liberal education. This classification system is therefore educationally valuable, because it shows graphically the difference in usage among signs, tools, models, and art forms. The six classes will provide the format for our discussions in the following chapters.

In diagrammatically cataloging the several possible ways that displacement activity functions in symbolic discourse, we have seen that torsion occurs as soon as coding makes one thing stand for another. Hence we see that the axiom of torsion, expressed first by Euclid, in reversing a line, a plane, etc., is not singly a geometrical phenomenon, but is also a radical of semiotic representation. This cataloged axiom could be useful, therefore, in working with a premise shared by scientists beginning with Francis Bacon, that all living activity is coded.

J. Z. Young, the neuroanatomist, however, has warned against the possible confusion that might occur when associating human semiotic conventions with other coded forms found in living activity. For instance, Young says that as symbols of the genetic code "the polynucleotide molecules serve to arrange the parts and actions of organisms so that they correspond to, or *represent*, their environment" (italics his).[43] So, for Young, an analogy with human communication codes is both advantageous and severely problematic, because one uses a speech code that is later in the evolutionary process in order to understand a hereditary code which is biologically more fundamental. Our diagrammed catalog should therefore be helpful in distinguishing torsion in human semiotic codes from the various kinds of foldings in the arrangements of DNA molecules. Similarly, the catalog might serve to separate the Euclidean geometries by which we construct signs, tools, and models from the generation of more or less symmetrical forms found in other living activity.

CHAPTER 1

Three-Dimensional Semiotics

... splitting and fusing the atom both derive, conceptually, from a discovery made in prehistory: that stone and all matter has a structure along which it can be split and put together in new arrangements.

J. Bronowski, *The Ascent of Man*

The epigraph yields a useful method for understanding signs of three-dimensional discovery.[1] A tandem method of cutting and then of recombining structures, accomplished by the precision of skilled hands, is the pattern to be explored in this chapter. For that pattern inheres both in crafting tools and in modeling hypotheses in three space. That twofold method is the semiotic pattern of deconstruction and then of subsequent reassemblage "on a different plane," as Lévi-Strauss expressed it. But as the epigraph further attests, the tandem semiosis is worked upon material that itself is patterned with a significant structure, a grain along which it is cut and reconstructed. We shall therefore attend to three-dimensional matter that yields an epistemological sense of patterned substructure, which in turn becomes a foundation or semiotic ground for subsequent super-structuring. First, however, we shall explore the idea of the crafting hand, for the sensory-motor qualities of 'handling' are crucial for the modeling of discoveries. Then too, the complementary fittingness of splitting and of fusing admit the possibility of classifying three-dimensional instruments into two different kinds: cutting tools such as knives, which do the work of analysis, and combining tools such as pots, which do the work of synthesis. If skills are achieved, as Michael Polanyi claims, "by alternate dismemberment and inte-

47

gration," an examination of this pattern must improve one's perspective upon three dimensional instruments.[2]

Encomium for Hands

"My hands," said the Centaur, "have felt rocks, waters, plants without number, and the subtlest impressions of atmosphere, for I lift up my hands on dark, still nights to detect the breezes and so discover signs to make sure of my way."
Henri Focillon, "In Praise of Hands,"
Life of Forms in Art

Perhaps the Centaur's 'groping' for sign is the most common metaphor for the prelude to discovery. In the dark, a trial and error of the hand feels its ways to understanding: touching, spanning, grasping. However, as a metaphorical state of incipience, 'groping' is a condition that one longs to replace with some larger law in logic, geometry, and semiotics, so that everyone need not repeat the particular instance of an apple falling on one's head. Groping is that wordless state, fraught with expectation, prior to the successful articulation of word, phrase, or formula. What properties of the hand made it so especially appropriate as a latent metaphor for the discovery of signs?

Images of hands imprinted in the clay wall galleries of the Aurignacian period represent the beginnings of primeval semiotics. Those silhouettes and pictures of hands are the earliest signs.[3] Their meaning is manifold, because their cauterization from the whole body signifies by that part a supplication for the whole. The hand signifies what it does: it gropes for and grasps other probes, and it reaches, in the fashion of Tantalus, for intangible connections with the whole. Being both utilitarian and magical, the hand's formative potential is represented on cave walls all over the world. In their earliest definition, therefore, hands draw attention to a hypothetical dimension of semiotics, one of evocation.

In his chapter "The Magic of the Hand," Max Raphael argues that for Paleolithic hunting cultures hands were intermediaries that magically symbolized a degree of control over animals, which were the measure of all things in that they supported hunting life.[4] He maintains that the proportion of the hand, the ratio of its length to width (3:2), was "the main source of compositional form in Paleolithic art" (p. 31). And following the argument of earlier historical linguists, he asserts that the reason why several hundred Indo-European roots have concrete meanings derived from bodily gestures, specifically those of the hand, is that the speaking organ imitated the sign language of hand movements (p. 32). Furthermore, the asymmetrical form of the outstretched hand gave it a freedom of movement and hence a heterogeneous function that displaced capabilities from the symmetry and limited place of those animals which represented nature.

The asymmetry of the human hand, by reason of the torsion of the opposing thumb, cannot be underemphasized, considering the wider implications of handedness in semiotic discourse. In J. Z. Young, *An Introduction to the Study of Man,* an essential section on tool making includes both a discussion of the evolution of the opposing thumb's precision grip at the dawning of *homo faber,* and an account of the "chipped-pebble culture" that resulted (Chapter 36). Hands, not eyes, define the phenomena of mass, weight, surface, and volume; this capacity for manipulating objects provides for Young the possibility of discussing a radical of classification. The world has an altogether different nature for animals that can pick up and analyze things than for those which merely move around in a static setting:

> We are too ignorant to say more but it may be that with handling came the beginning of other classes of objects, and their classification. With using and then actually shaping them came further development of whatever groupings of cells and activities in the brain provide the internal representations that allow "thinking" about them and, either before or after this, naming.[5]

Apart from evolutionary issues in neurophysiology, there can be isolated here the fittingness of the hand's capacity for three-dimensional classification. Asymmetrical in itself and asymmetrical in its opposition of left and right, the hand has a capacity for cleaving and for molding matter into structural patterns that begins a romance with symmetry which extends to the furthest 'reaches of' cosmology and microbiology.[6]

Abstract Objects

In the highly ritualized cultures of both east and west there exist parables of the wise man, distanced by implements that have become impediments rather than aids, who returns for guidance to a 'primitive' craftsman's first principles of discovery. In Chinese culture the most famous example of what has been called "knack technology" is the tale about the butcher of the Prince of Hui who does not work with his eyes.[7] Governed by hand and mind, his chopper seeks significant patterns in the carcass; it finds the interstices, joints, and crevices. In so doing, his chopper never needs to be sharpened. "For where the parts join there are interstices, and since the edge of the chopper has no thickness, one can easily insert it into them." After watching his butcher, the prince exclaims that he now knows how to nourish life. The Prince, a Confucian statesman, derives his ideas of maintenance and endurance from Taoist primitivism: there is complementary fittingness in matching a tool with the structural lines of force in an object. As we noticed with regard to Bronowski's passage about splitting and fusing the atom, analytic cutting is followed by a recombination of structural units into new codes of use.

In this process, hand-held tools are no longer construed to be utilitarian means to a different end, but rather as metaphorical ways of rediscovering simplicity through pervasive pattern. "Cleave the wood, and I am there," says one of the Christian logia, rediscovered early in this century.[8] The same kind of palingenetic return to simplicity was the beginning of the crafts movement in the history of Western education. Jean Jacques Rousseau's student Emile would have only one book from age twelve to fifteen, and it would be *Robinson Crusoe,* whose isolated career on that tropical island seemed to recapitulate, for Rousseau, the course of civilization, beginning with the simplest crafting of tools. Therefore, before age twelve Emile would work only with his hands, primarily in carpentry. Then he would learn to distrust these arts which are perfected by "subdivision, by the infinite multiplication of tools."[9]

Laying aside Rousseau's ideological predelictions, one can agree that the issue involves a by-product of ritualization, where the very process of abstraction is seen as dross. How can this be? Abstraction is the translation process at the very heart of semiosis, certainly; for all signs, tools, and models are abstractions in at least two ways. The first is that spatial paradox which renders the sign magical for primitive humans. As Giedion says, "symbolization arose from the need to give perceptible form to the imperceptible."[10] By abstracting, that is, by conventionalizing the natural features of a bison, a carving or a painting evoked the absent beast as an icon. A few signatures—the meaty hump, the heavy shoulders, the lyrelike horns, the gravid outline—symbolize by parts the absent whole. Or to reverse it, the creature is not present when the object is featured. This spatialized form of abstraction—in Latin *abstrahere,* "to drag away," "to divert"—forms the basis of substitution magic. But early humans were apparently more oriented toward the temporal process of abstraction: tools and signs were implements of planning, of anticipation magic, where making the implement deferred immediate gratification in order to concentrate on a future goal. According to Young, the physiological emergence of *Homo sapiens* depends upon this temporal form of abstraction. The functions of the frontal lobe are summarized as "the maintenance of the proper balance between action and restraint, and the capacity to form actions for which the reward is delayed"[11] Young follows R. J. Pumphrey in suggesting that "this power of abstraction is related to the development of the power of planning several stages of action in the future, and so to the development of language" (p. 538).

Ritualized objects can therefore be viewed both as spatial as well as temporal abstractions which foreshorten different dimensions. But in almost any temporal series of abstractions the means and ends vary so that abstraction is the end product of the process. Consider the ritualized development of stone tools. 'Dawn stones' are so rudely chipped that it is often difficult to ascertain whether they have been accidentally or purposefully broken. Beginning with three-dimensional objects, where intentionality is obscure, classification of flint implements proceeds upon the basis of increasing symmetry in the designs upon the blades, and also upon increasingly sophisticated methods of achieving that design. One of the most significant shifts in method was the construction of intermediate tools in order to make tools. The inventing of "burins," for example, small flakes that were used as punches, yielded a process called "pressure flaking," instead of percussion, which resulted in much more efficient and elegant blades. Young summarizes this abstracting feat of *Homo sapiens sapiens* in terms of what we have called means-ends analysis. "The achievement of a goal was sought by increasingly indirect methods" (p. 508).

Farther along in the series of abstractions, efficiency and elegance part company from Ting the butcher, when we observe that the beauty of the flaking and the rarity of the material result in purely symbolic jade halberds found in Chinese tombs. A further shift toward increasing abstraction, popular in the history of numismatics, involves a foreshortening of Chinese "knife" money. It provides a credible theory for the origin of round coins. In addition to bronze arrow-point tokens shaped like dragons, there were *tao* or knife coins with long blades and round handles. The theory supposes that the inconvenience of handling prompted the shortening of the blade and the puncturing of the round handle so that they might be put together on a string. "Finally the blade disappeared entirely leaving only the circular handle with a hole in the center."[12] Were it not for extant forms in the series, like the species of dance fly which offers an empty balloon, it would be difficult to conjecture a coinlike placebo. In other words, an abstraction process dematerializes the three-dimensional properties of substance in favor of reading two-dimensional axes of pattern and form, ending in an almost purely abstract sign of counting units that could be strung together in a unidimensional sequence. That kind of three-dimensional cutting tool has been so ritualized that mathematical 'cuts' are all that remain. They have ceased to be three-dimensional tools that cut other objects, but are now three-dimensional abstractions that analyze the hypothetical dimension in denominations. As with the butcher's chopper, these edges have no thickness.

It may be that this popular theory is fallacious, because round coins may have been in use even before knife coins were invented. If that is the case, then the evidence of the series, that is, the actual sequence in coinage, becomes less important than the persistence of the theory in time. The popularity of the theory underlines a willfulness to make objects conform to a temporal process of increasing abstraction, of ritualization.

Cutting Tools

According to the pattern of splitting and fusing with which the chapter opened, cutting tools comprise half the class of A instruments (those which highlight three-dimensional, torque two-dimensional, and suppress one-dimensional aspects), the other kind being combining tools. These two kinds are complementary, just as mortar and pestle are representatives of the two different kinds of class A instruments that in functioning fit together. Cutting tools are always figures, while combining tools are always grounds. If all figural tools operate on an apparently undifferentiated ground, it therefore follows that an instrument's complementary ground is the hypothetical dimension, being a figure's potential locus of operation. Consider the well-known example of being blindfolded and of probing a room with a stick. For Niels Bohr that psychological phenomenon emblematizes the reciprocal character of his theory of complementarity.[13] For when one handles the stick loosely, it seems to the sense of touch to be a foreign object, separate from the subject; but when the stick is grasped firmly, the haptic sense shifts down to the end of the stick and seems to be localized where one taps or probes another object. Just as classical mechanics demands the separation of space and time, so does classical philosophy demand the separation of subject and object, while the conventions of classical language underscore both kinds of separation. But in Bohr's view the natural interference of what we have called a figure-ground relationship is the more demanding problem that has been compounded by virtue of classical conventions: "It would scarcely be an exaggeration to maintain, purely from psychological experiences [such as the stick experiment], that the concepts of space and time by their very nature acquire a meaning only because of the possibility of neglecting the inter-action with the means of measurement" (p. 99).

It is instructive that the most elementary three-dimensional tool, a probing stick, can become a way of explaining some of the more 'abstract' twentieth-century physical theories. In their radical simplicity, implements of three dimensions highlight a material dimension rather than suppress it. They therefore seem to 'incorporate' the thingliness of nature better than conceptual tools, which delineate a metaphysical world.

The complementarity of the probe results from handling it firmly. Then, as Michael Polanyi expresses it, the stick is no longer an exosomatic instrument but has become "internalized,"[14] thereby establishing a bridge with the other side. Although the stick is firmly vectoral, it receives messages about the hypothetical dimension, as well as sends them. The ground of its operation serves as a tympanum, while the figural probe transmits and receives. As a two-way bridge, figuring complementarity, it works like Jakob von Uexküll's *Funktionskreis,* a circular system of receptors and effectors that will be examined in Chapter 4.

In most simple cutting tools the reciprocity between it and its complementary ground is suppressed. The 'object' or 'point' is to use the cutting tool as a wedge or unidirectional vector, splitting the object along its grain. And the wedge is usually attached to a wooden handle that is itself longitudinally cut with its own lines of force, which strengthens the handle by reducing reciprocal shock, and therefore impeding unwanted reverse signals. Unlike signs and models which assume a human recipient and therefore a mutual translation of sound and sense, as in speech signs, tools are not designed to highlight reciprocity. Because they analyze and split, as a student once exclaimed, wedges must emblematize a "divide and conquer" philosophy. As we shall see in Chapter 4, analytic probing is often seen as the method of reductionism; and holism, its necessary complement, utilizes synthetic methods.

Combining Tools

The signboard quality of the pointing hand is so much a part of our visual code that, in thinking of it as a vectoral probe, one might ignore the facility of the hand for being transformed into a cup.[15] The class of container implements torques the two-dimensional plane so that it curves into three space, with a resulting barrier betwixt inside and outside. The class incorporates a grammar of molds that makes it more suitable for models of theory than the class of figural probes. As the asymmetrical complement to the pestle, the mortar is the ground or foundation of action. All upgathering things spring from and return to it, as this surprisingly appropriate medieval quiddity suggests:

> Erthe out of erthe is wonderly wrought;
> Erthe hath of erthe a dignity of nought:
> Erthe upon erthe has set all his thought
> How that erthe upon erthe may be heigh brought.

As with the Babylonian *apsu* and the Grecian *apeiron,* earth is the apparently undifferentiated building stuff upon which earthen figures walk. But here the medieval theologian reverses the inconsistency of logical types. Ordinarily one suppresses from consideration the components of a test tube so that one can attend to ingredients inside the container; ordinarily one ignores the material components of a pointing hand in order to understand the directed object. In the pride of their wonderful figures, human beings tend to ignore their earthly components, which they only seem to transcend. By denying discrimination of names and signs and by subsuming all into the class "erthe," the theologian highlights, without naming it 'vanity', the condition of ignoring the building stuff.

Such earthly foundations are crucial in epistemology; even the term *episteme* is derived from a root of 'firmness' or 'stability'.[16] Epistemology therefore seems to require an invisible platform, a suppressed understanding, from which further discovery leaps. The philosophy of founding is Martin Heidegger's *Urgrund,* that primal foundation on which being stands.[17] It is for him the "fundamental" question, because it involves considering both the absence of ground, the abyss, as well as the apparent necessity of ground. Heidegger's process of "disclosure," the making visible of unnoticed foundations, is modern philosophy's entrant in a large interdisciplinary movement to discover invariants underlying and unaffected by the many transformational variants of a discipline.[18]

Unfortunately the structural metaphor of "underlying" can be conceptually misleading, as Emmon Bach has pointed out.[19] For it is the slippery stepping stone of Baconian induction. Bach observes that the phrase "based on," appearing in such statements as "science must be based on observation and experiment," derives metaphorically from the geometry of pyramids (p. 17). The phrase implicitly underlies Bacon's own description in Aphorism CIV of the *Novum Organon:*

> But then, and only then, may we hope well of the sciences when in a just scale of ascent, and by successive steps not interrupted or broken, we rise from particulars to lesser axioms; and then to middle axioms, one above the other; and last of all to the most general. . . .
> The understanding must not therefore be supplied with wings, but rather hung with weights, to keep it from leaping and flying.

For Bach such creative "leaps" to discovery are Keplerian rather than Baconian and are more to be relied on in linguistic study than the Baconian model. For "foundations do not exist." Despite our own emphasis upon semiotic leaps, we shall not follow Bach's uncurbed approach. On the contrary, Chapter 4 will explain that induction and deduction are complementary approaches, both of which interact with one another, as wings hung with weights.

The more immediate task is to understand the principle of foundations as they are associated with combining tools. Both Raphael and Giedion maintain that there is no baseline in paleolithic art; Raphael says, "The invention of the horizontal modeling line marks the birth of autonomous art in prehistoric Egypt."[20] The neolithic pots illustrated in Figure 11, from Raphael, have an intrinsic geometry, an observed baseline. Because

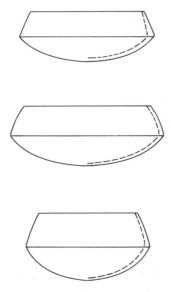

FIG. 11. Tracings of three early Egyptian pots which
feature a horizontal axis.

they had no conception of horizonality or verticality, paleolithic
creators wrought with a "multidirectional liberty" that is analogous to the conceptual freedom of Cubism or any other modern
movement that feels imprisoned in Euclidean space.[21] But Egyptian pottery signifies a point of departure, where all art is now
related to the vertical dimension of bilateral symmetry, with hori-
zontals of ninety degrees considered as by-products of the vertical.

The new demands of neolithic industry were the apparent
formal causes of this new geometrical symmetry. For in the static
industries of settled communities that characterized the neolithic
period, there began warp-and-woof geometries of weaving cloth
and baskets, as well as the stacking principles of building stones
upon stones in habitable symmetry. For Raphael, the shift from
multidimensional liberty to vertical limitations had its analog in

the shift from communal hunting cultures to hierarchically organized universal states, where vertical castes and horizontal communication systems replaced the undifferentiated denizens of the meandering game trail (Chapter 1). This ideological argument is not easily set aside, if only because it depends upon the powerful symmetries of the baseline analogy.

Whether it be in the laying of bricks in different designs, or in the laying of roof tiles according to different patterns, all such are examples of the idea that stacking is a three-dimensional classification. To formulate a baseline, to make a first distinction, is to begin to construct a system of close packing, where everything fits into an orderly mosaic. That apparent separation of efficiency from waste became early in history a hypothetical substitute for thinking about the structure of a world. The real secret of the Great Pyramid is to figure how it can incorporate in its limited structure so many different theories about what it 'stands' for, that is, about what 'understands' it.

For Napoleon Bonaparte's surveyors, the Great Pyramid became an excellent geodetic benchmark for mapping the earth surrounding it.[22] Once they saw that the four corners of the pyramid coincided with the cardinal points of the compass, they were then able to use the meridian running through its apex as the baseline for their subsequent mapping. Apart from its theological significance and aside from its mathematical mysticism— that its various features can be construed to serve for models of *pi* and the Golden Section or *phi*—the pyramid served as a practical *gnomon* for cartographers many centuries later, just as it had served as a T-square millennia earlier for measuring local acreage. As a measure of the earth it became a symbol of the land; hence these first monumental geometers initiated a powerful 'base' for subsequent epistemology. What else is a gnomon other than a combining tool, the L-shaped border of the carpenter's rule, that provides a base for further deployment? Gnomons are instruments of pure ratio and proportion, but their very dematerialization can serve to remind that a pyramid of solid building blocks bolsters every abstracted right triangle that is drawn or thought about. This is both the advantage and the limitation of combining tools used as models; they can serve as Archimedian fulcra by which to move a world, yet they can also be deployed too exclusively as hypothetical building blocks, especially when the question of unexamined a priori or 'basic' assumptions needs to be disclosed for analysis.

There exists in the use of three-dimensional combining tools, such as pyramids, one of the earliest and yet most continuous forms of semiotic confusion. The mistake arises when one substitutes three-dimensional objects for the hypothetical dimension. Consider that when one is reading a map, he doesn't confuse the real space that the map inhabits with the symbolic space of the terrain to which it refers: "While a map itself exists and occupies space, it derives its meaning and usefulness from the fact that it represents some other space."[23] By virtue of a dimensional reduction to a two-dimensional plane, the interpreter more readily discriminates real from symbolic terrain. Because a crafted three-dimensional object does not have the advantage of a dimensional reduction, it is easier to confuse the real space in which it is set with the symbolic space, or hypothetical dimension, to which it refers. For example, in many archaic cultures, if a craftsman carves a box or folds it from leather hides and then depicts on the several sides of the box the matching perspectives of an animal, then the box becomes the animal. As Claude Lévi-Strauss says of the chests of Northwest Coast art, they are "not merely containers embellished with a printed or carved animal. They are the animal itself, keeping an active watch over the ceremonial ornaments which have been entrusted to its care."[24] This collapse of 'real' three-dimensional space into symbolic space, where there is less observed torsion between different dimensions, gives rise to the substitution magic of Pygmalion's beloved emerging from sculpted "erthe." Similarly, the upgathering power from the land of the pyramid transforms the 3D model into a genius 'incorporating' *pi,* or the Golden Section *phi;* that is, abstract building blocks of mathematics entwined with geometry. Objects formulated 'in the round' are so completely delimited, so autonomous, that the surround must gather around it, making it a perspectival omphallos, no matter what its structure otherwise may be.

All of nature exists 'in the round'. The ability of hands to pick up and to handle, to begin as Young says a rudimentary process of three-dimensional classification, suggests that objects are separable from their environs. The separability, for instance, of flint or amber from its native strains allows the demographic charting of prehistoric trade routes. Only humans transfer such material to other use, and their distance from origin can be ascertained. So natural objects that have been exchanged, for whatever use, are not 'really' natural; instead they are used 'in' a fictive or hypothetical dimension separable from their original grounds. Our caution about imitating nature with three-dimensional models of discovery is therefore a variation upon Galileo's caveat, cited in his Introduction: "what will be so wonderful in imitating 'sculptress nature' by sculpture itself, in representing that which is relieved by relief itself?" In this regard, a better mirror of nature is a plane, because it reminds one that an accommodation is being made. A dimensional reduction reminds the modeler that his design has different intentionality than the matter he hopes to solve, for nature makes no predictions.

One does not make this dimensional semiotic mistake in the ordinary application of containing tools. One does not confuse the contents of a test tube with the container. But in archaic modeling and apparently in some contemporary accounts of modeling, one too hastily throws the baby, the bathwater, plus the container, into a confused metaphor. In other words, the substitution of three-dimensional objects for the hypothetical dimension of symbolic space creates the possibility of logical error. Although three-dimensional objects match the requirements that our brains need for thinking of nature in three dimensions, the equivalence of one with another may give rise to an illogical mixture: "She came home in a flood of tears and a sedan chair." Understanding these limitations of three-dimensional models allows one to make more discerning use of their many advantages.

But whence arises this illogic in the first place? As with all other good and bad ideas, it occurs in the sudden association of ideas. As Thomas Hobbes said, "Thought is quick."[25] For Hobbes, words have no material, no three-dimensional, substance; hence we are duped into making fanciful linguistic associations such as "incorporeal body" or "round quadrangle" (p. 20). But we should not confuse these sudden, unguided products of our fancy with reason about natural objects. Hobbes concludes,

> The Light of humane minds is Perspicuous Words, but by exact definitions first snuffed, and purged from ambiguity; *Reason* is the *pace;* Increase of *Science* the way; and Benefit of *man-kind,* the *end.* And on the contrary, Metaphors, and senseless words are like *ignes fatui* . . . (p. 26).

For our purposes the will of the wisp to be avoided here is the unintentional shift in dimensions between words and things; the yoking of two dissimilars such as "incorporeal body" produces monsters not angels. The materialist Hobbes is attacking scholastic theologians who infested nature with insubstantial creatures of their own fancy, but we make the same mistake if we confuse the hypothetical dimension of three space with the 'real' world of three space.

"Open, Barley!"

Ali Baba's brother, Cassim, learned to his peril that the difference between the outside and the inside of a three-dimensional model is the difference between storage and retrieval of information. Once Cassim was inside the cave, he was so bewildered by the rich information stored there that he forgot the code which would unlock the door, which would let him retrieve the treasure, and so escape the thieves. Container models are radicals of semiotic transfer, such as ships, because they are classic exosomatic instruments. They store information outside the body, and so, as J. Z. Young observes, exosomatic instruments duplicate functions that were originally limited to endosomatic instruments:

> Written records are, like all other tools, an artificial substitute for a function that was previously performed in the body—in this case by the chromosomes of the germ cells. As has happened with other tools the invention of the capacity to make extra-somatic memory records in written codes has led eventually to an understanding of the code in the body.[26]

Cassim reminds one, perforce, that in order to retrieve the coded treasure within, a different code must be used, as Young is using information theory. Both "treasure" and "sesame" are codes that work in identical fashion. They are contracts fashioned in one medium that are enforced to stand for another pattern of events; thus 'treasure' buys grain and other sustenance; and 'sesame' retrieves treasure. But the codes are not reversible. Outsides and insides work by analogous but different codes. Inside one is in the presence of stored information, but outside one needs to retrieve.

Does our use of "Ali Baba and the Forty Thieves" mean that it was written as an allegory about information theory? By no means. Even if one defines allegory as a narrative sequence where one pattern of events is contracted to stand in the place of another pattern, even then we have merely redefined the semiotic pattern of exchange-with-displacement. Our fascination with the story springs from its setting. It contains the classic "locked room" of "The Purloined Letter," "Murders in the Rue Morgue," and so many other stories of detection. Setting is the ground for action, and a locked room defies the efforts of everyday logic to find the key, to enter it, and to make outside accord with inside. In all such stories the 'key' is distortive conjecture. For example, we have transferred the story of Ali Baba from one category of use to another; we have given it a new association of ideas by taking it outside of its context of a thousand and one Arabian nights and have associated it generally with three-dimensional thresholds inside which we wish to probe. In locked-room puzzles, the key is the *turn* itself. But perhaps the conjecture is a Hobbesian *ignis fatuus,* for we have associated a specifically fictive locked cave with 'real' three–dimensional models which one can handle. Nevertheless, those models of discovery that one can touch and probe into are also fictive inventions, because they remain hypothetical searches for keys or codes.

Three-dimensional container models allow one to see and to handle outsides and insides simultaneously. They transform locked rooms or "black boxes" into visible skeletons. Black boxes are conceptual devices that remind one explicitly that the contents and processes inside the hypothetical problem are not known and cannot be tampered with.[27] What we have called models are called in the parlance of systems analysis "white boxes." Gerald Weinberg explains that white boxes simulate the hypothetical problem in exactly the opposite way to black boxes (pp. 171–72). Black boxes perceptually and conceptually remind one that the innards of a system are concealed in impenetrability, while white boxes serve as three-dimensional reconstructions that approximate as exactly as the theory permits the revealed inner workings of a problem. Black boxes explicitly suppress the chief advantages of three-dimensional white-box models; they deny kinesthetic orientation of contents into significant patterns. White boxes, or models, as they will continue to be called here, allow the trial-and-error construction of an anatomy. All other systems not under analysis and construction are pared away so that only one pattern is highlighted. For example, if one wanted to construct a three-dimensional model of the nervous system of a cat, the other overlapping systems, such as muscles or skeleton, would be suppressed, or included only insofar as they link with or form armatures for the nerve-cell patterns.

Three-dimensional container models therefore reverse the ordinary patterns of insides and outsides of real space in favor of a modified and modifiable symbolic space. With three-dimensional models one can 'handle' symbolic space. By means of substitution magic one makes the inside of a problem perceptible to the eye and removes the problem to a model in real space that is modifiable by the hand, so that it signifies the inside has become outside. Or conversely, that one has gone into the interior, bringing the outside in: "Open, Sesame!" That pattern approximates the ideal with which we opened, that skills are learned by alternating dismemberment and reassemblage, and that learning itself is a variant of dynamic memory, involving both the storage and the retrieval of information.

Class A Anatomy

Class A instruments highlight three-dimensional, torque two-dimensional, and suppress one-dimensional aspects. Class D instruments highlight three-dimensional, torque one-dimensional, and suppress two-dimensional aspects, but Class D will be discussed at large in Chapter 4, since the inclusion of one-dimensional aspects such as time, movement, and sequence in the object renders it into a spatio-temporal 'whole' system, not just an object. Although the movement of the crafting hand is crucial in the construction of three-dimensional semiotic objects, although the modifying hand is necessary for rearranging building blocks of material, and although the wielding hand is never very far from semiosis in three space, nevertheless a semblance of movement has no part in Class A instruments. Perhaps because movement is suppressed in many three-dimensional objects, the sensory-motor motions of conceptual thinking are often ignored in discussions of discovery. To what extent are the kinesthetic-haptic qualities of the crafting hand appropriate to the sophisticated task of building models of discovery? Are sensory-motor capabilites merely rudimentary or primitive skills, belonging to the same class of habitual skills as the ability to button one's shirt buttons without looking or thinking about the process? Not when one considers that the sensory-motor act of 'handling' has topological immediacy. In three-dimensional building, the crucial discernment is what might be called "placement logic." The physical actions, the muscular facility of arrangement and rearrangement, are topological coordinations of three-dimensional building blocks in neighborhoods, corridors, boundaries.

Sensory-motor intelligence, for Jean Piaget, begins in the child a logic of ordering and of correspondences that "are the foundations for the logical mathematical structures."[28] He has observed that in the development of a child's conceptual thinking, the latest kind of geometry developed in history, the topological, is the earliest development in the child. For the child's topological conception of moving objects in space precedes an understanding of Euclidean conventions such as straight lines, planes, and circles (p. 31). In the child, "the first intuitions are topological." This "practical logic of sensory-motor intelligence" is the foundation of subsequent conceptual thinking, because from ages one and one-half to eight it becomes "internalized" in practice. But for Piaget a "semiotic function" of representation replaces the actual carrying out of actions during those years (p. 45). He groups, as we do here, all re-presentations of actions under semiosis: gestures (both idiosyncratic and systematized), drawing, painting, modeling, even mental imagery, as well as language. By means of sensory-motor intelligence, Piaget argues, one can avoid Noam Chomsky's dependence upon an innate kernel of invariance, from which linguistic transformations vary (pp. 47–48). Although that argument veers from our present scrutiny, it nevertheless suggests the importance to Piaget of topological handling, since he is an admirer of Chomsky's revolutionary thinking in linguistics.

Topological handling of significant shapes and their representation, as well as the three-dimensional classification of stacking blocks carved from the more Euclidean conventions, therefore become early internalized molds for thinking about the structures of a child's world. Although one of the platitudes about discovery involves seeing with the eye of the child through the experienced maturity of wisdom, surely there is some analogy between the initial discoveries of children and the first discoveries of wise adults. Fairy tales, Mother Goose, the Alice stories, even Winnie the Pooh, are favorite detours of physicists, mathematicians, cosmologists, linguists, and other humanists of the liberal arts, all those who wish to look afresh, from radical perspectives, at problems of symmetrical form and of skewed sense.

Given the suppression of this important movement in the construction and handling of Class A instruments, let us consider more systematically the re-presentation of objects in the symbolic space of a hypothetical dimension. For real objects such as Tinker Toys are re-presented, that is, coded to new symbolic uses, even as their three-dimensionality in real space is highlighted. The round wheels and straight sticks become nodes and armatures of any anatomical problem of the hypothetical dimension.

Anyone who would highlight three-dimensional models of discovery must acknowledge the importance of James D. Watson and Francis Crick's model of a double helix for structuring DNA. For the scientific legitimacy of modeling as a rigorous enterprise was no longer questioned following the representation of that process of discovery. Watson says that until their successful formulation, some colleagues barely disguised their scorn, because model building was seen as the "easy resort of slackers who wanted to avoid the hard work necessitated by an honest scientific career."[29] With that model, furthermore, science and semiotics joined hands, because DNA is the instructional unit for communicating genetic information. It is the radical invariant of biology. And according to Sebeok, "The genetic code must be regarded as the most fundamental of all semiotic networks and therefore as the prototype for all other signaling systems used by animals, including man."[30]

Watson suspected that since most biological phenomena occur in pairs, their spiral model should have two strands. So he began to construct a placement logic, based on a figural simile, which featured a spiral staircase that had bonded horizontal steps connecting the two external backbone spirals. Here Watson and Crick conjectured a double helix upon which to string several chemical components. Not the least important part of the model was the insight that the two spiral strands were not identical in structure, but rather were complementary. So as each strand divided in cellular reproduction it would serve as a "mold" or "template" for the new strand, "like a lock to a key," as Watson put it (pp. 84, 125, 135). The three-dimensional similes are stressed here because they work as parallel modes of discourse that reinforce both the process of discovery, as in the spiral staircase, and the process of communicating to others, as in the lock and key. They are not to be construed as exact isomorphs, but rather as analogies, just as one uses the codes of human communication theory to understand a hereditary code that is "biologically more fundamental than the human speech code," as Young cautions.[31] Perhaps the most crucial parallel of semiotic discourse that Watson and Crick had at their disposal for interpreting and confirming their model was the x-ray photograph, a two-dimensional pictograph.

No effort was made to incorporate movement in that three-dimensional model, even though the hands of the inventors were crucial in modifying relationships of the several molecular bases in order to see where and, therefore, how they stacked symmetrically. Although that suppression of movement accords with the classification of Class A instruments, there was also no explicit effort to torque two-dimensional aspects. Torsion cannot be explicit; it cannot be highlighted, because it is characterized by the obliquity of the push-pull phenomenon. In the Introduction torsion was defined as a visualizable awareness of deflection that occurs in the use of semiotic instruments when an object is 'accommodated' from one category of use to another. So in decoding the model of DNA one must look from the three-dimensional aspects of the solid struts in real space to their meaning 'in' the hypothetical dimension. One must also recall that according to conventional drawing practices in chemistry, the struts are organized in pentagons or hexagons, but the several atoms which organize the molecular structure in geometrical relationships are not included.[32] In order to draw attention to architectonics rather than individual atoms, the nodes or wheels of the tinker-toy assemblage are assumed but not depicted. When one generalizes that in Class A instruments a semblance of two-dimensionality is torqued, one can say that many three-dimensional constructs depend for their use upon a two-dimensional convention also. It is a convention, of course, because nature does not 'see' things at all, much less in a two-dimensional aspect. However, when human beings see things from an external perspective, from outside the object, that perspective is usually reified into a two-dimensional plane. As we shall see in Chapter 2, this 'side view' of objects (where a brick wall, for instance, exhibits a simultaneous side view of symmetrical stacking as well as a diachronic recipe for three-dimensional stacking) has a number of planar permutations that must be clearly itemized.

Conclusion

It is important to recall that crafted three-dimensional objects are semiotic conventions, just as is three-dimensionality, or dimensionality itself. Any represented form is merely a static semblance of a transition in a quantum situation, whether it be

a cross section or a three-dimensional *tableau vivant*. We therefore subscribe to John Dewey's argument that symmetry is static
rhythm. Any art form is a structural cross section of rhythmic
continuity.[33] Any "dimension" is really a geometrization into
point, line, plane, or solid of some conventional aspect of patterned flux. We reify fluxion into complements of space and time
or subject and object in order to gauge their dimensional magnitude. So our conventional division of semiosis into six categories,
of which Class A is the first to be described, is more accurate than
three dimensions, because it shows the conspicuous attitudes of
torsion itself as the object folds towards expansion or duration.
Put another way, the six categories are symmetrical arrangements
of the various manifestations of semiotic torsion. So the suppression of movement in Class A instruments reinforces the illusion
that this kind of three-dimensional object is absolutely static,
except when manipulated by the classifying hand.

As with the various examples of skulls used in the Introduction, this method of describing signs, tools, and models contin-
ues to be perspectivist. We subscribe to an idea of Henri
Bergson's that is similar to Dewey's cited above:

> Now, life is an evolution. We concentrate a period of this evolution
> in a stable view which we call a form, and, when the change has
> become considerable enough to overcome the fortunate inertia of
> our perception, we say that the body has changed its form. But in
> reality the body is changing form at every moment; or rather, there
> is no form, since form is immobile and the reality is movement.
> What is real is the continual *change* of form: *form is only a snapshot view
> of a transition* (italics his).[34]

An example more acute than the use of skulls is the craft of
knotting, because that craft, and its theory, focuses upon the
dimensionality of transitional states. In *The Child's Conception of
Space,* Jean Piaget and Barbel Inhelder conducted a series of
experiments with young children in order to test their ability to

discern and to tie overhand knots.[35] Here we shall be less concerned with their results concerning the development of topological awareness than with their premises about the dimensionality of knots. A piece of rope, or 'line' as it is called in nautical terminology, is a nice expression of one-dimensionality. When the line is turned toward itself in an arc and then connected in a circle, then that transition defines a two-dimensional surface characterized by inside-outside elements of separation and connection. And the act of turning the line back upon itself, over and under, amounts to a three-dimensional transition. Now it was precisely this "transition from one dimension to another, within one and the same object" that made the tieing of an overhand knot so difficult for young children to perform (p. 111).

What is difficult about this kind of dimensional transition? Perhaps it has the quality of things apparently self-evident. Perhaps it has the same kind of familiarity as one of the pioneer meditations of Gestalt psychology, that once a line drawn on a piece of paper begins to close, we no longer see a line against a background; instead we see a surface figure bounded by a line. In explaining the difficulty of transitional states, Piaget and Inhelder define it as a special kind of betweenness. For instance, in any three elements A B C arranged in a linear series, the element B expresses a special quality of order expressed by the word "between." This betweenness they express as a special instance of the more general topological quality of "surrounding":

> If the location of a point 'between' two others designates a one-dimensional surrounding (defining a line), and the location of a point inside or outside a closed figure . . . designates a two-dimensional surrounding (defining a surface); then the relationship of a point, whether inside or outside a closed box, designates a three-dimensional surrounding (defining a space) (p. 104).

This topological characterization has special application for students of semiotics because it provides us with a perspective upon a class of three-dimensional objects that express between-ness, a metaphorical bridging. (Recall that Bottom's Wall is a radical of semiotic separation and connection, of mediation.) We have said that there are two kinds of tools and models—cutting and combining or analytic and synthetic—and that the complementary process of analyzing and synthesizing defines a skill. As with the example of pestle and mortar, these figure-ground combinations allow latent sexual connotations. Phallic and vulvar joining is an archetype of much three-dimensional betweenness, simply because nature itself has been prodigal in using sexual jointure to get on with the business of maintaining the gene pool. So let us use the Latin word *copula* in order to define Class A instruments that exemplify the transitional state of 'between'.

That group would include hinges, bridges, lintels, all overhand knots, and their variations. The group of copulative objects are radicals of semiotic transfer, of exchange with displacement. For example, knots are flexible copulae that can result in a one-dimensional line of significant knots used in archaic counting practices, or a knotted fishing net that seems two-dimensional, or a woven basket which folds over into three space. These examples, illustrated by Figure 12, provide different perspectives upon betweenness with regard to their surrounding environs: copulae in one-dimensional intervals, in two-dimensional outsides and insides, and in three-dimensional arrangements over and under. In all cases, boundaries are surmounted and new surroundings reached by a transitional series of three-dimensional stacking and folding.

So what we have called 'torsion' is that transitional semblance of betweenness that governs the spatio-temporal enterprise. Copulative objects that we construct are our perspectival attempts to simulate similar jointures in nature. Knotting, for instance, shares interesting topological similarities with the folded structure of proteins.[36] Hence an important result of folding in the natural world is an increase of surface area within the

between   inside-outside   over-and-under

FIG. 12. Three representations of Betweenness. "Between" is one-dimensional in its linearity. "Inside-Outside" is two-dimensional when a circumscription of space implies a plane. "Over and Under" is three-dimensional when the first two possibilities are interwoven.

confines of minimal space. We have said before that every act of limitation implies a transcendence. But in the case of a boundary enclosing a locked room the transcendence occurs via folding patterns within the closed space. From our perspective of transitional folds, therefore, what we call a stomach may be viewed as a series of kinks that have evolved from a rudimentary gullet by way of the formal cause of pressure. In our bodies, furthermore, joints of various kinds, ligatures such as ligaments and synapses, are evolutionary results of 'experiments' with betweenness. As with any other semiotic object of mediation, they separate and connect two boundaries of different media.

In concluding this chapter, let us consider one final three-dimensional object; because, before going further, we must discriminate between two aspects of 'transition'. On the one hand copulae connect two elements in space. For purposes of transmitting signals, for instance, in the series *a, b, c,* it does not matter whether the series begins with *a* or *c; b* is still 'between'. From the perspective of evolution in time, however, any copula in nature could undergo various permutations; so a certain kind of ball and socket joint in this regard is a more or less successful transition in spatio-temporal development. Copulae are both exponents and critiques of evolutionary transition. But if there exists a semblance of transitional movement 'in' a constructed sign, tool, or model, then we have classified it, not as Class A, but as Class D. So let us close this chapter with a three-dimensional model of discovery which is clearly a copula, but which also includes a semblance of movement in its structure. This example must serve to allay one's expectations and questions about Class D instruments until they are enumerated in Chaper 4.

In that chapter we shall have occasion to mention the poet Goethe's flight to Italy, which amounts to a voyage of discovery for him. Consider, for now, this curious passage; it contains our final example:

> By means of levers and rollers it is possible to transport loads of considerable weight; to move the pieces of the obelisque it was necessary to use winches, pulleys, etc. The heavier the load or the greater the precision required of a thing—take a clock, for example —the more complicated or ingenious the mechanism has to be and, at the same time, the more perfect the unity of its internal structure. The same is true of all hypotheses, or rather, all *general principles.* The person who has nothing much to move grabs the lever and scorns my pulley; what can the stonemason do with an endless screw? . . .
>
> During the metaphysical discussions, I have often noticed with silent amusement that "they" did not take me seriously. Being an artist, I don't care. It might suit me much better if the principle upon which I work remains a secret. By all means, let them stick to their lever; I have been using my endless screw for a long time now and shall go on using it with ever greater ease and delight.[37]

Nowhere else in the *Journey* does Goethe mention this screw, but everywhere he looks for the Primal Plant, the solution to which would allow him to derive a larger principle of "metamorphosis" (p. 365). In the history of plant morphology Goethe's work with metamorphosis and spiral theory has been praised as forming the groundwork for a true science; and the principles of *phyllotaxis,* of leaf arrangement, especially in spiral staircases, derive from Goethe's thinking.[38] But were we not ourselves students of an emerging natural history of signs, this odd passage might make little sense. A screw is a cutting tool that is *turned* in a right or left-handed spiral to bore a hole or to connect two boundaries of wood. And when Goethe contemplated the tool as a model of discovery, he imagined the screw in operation. The element of movement 'in' the model renders it a Class D instrument. We shall consider spirals as dialectical models of discovery in Chapter 4. But for now consider that when a screw bores a hole by turning one way, it brings back to the surface the waste chips that have been probed away. And when the bit is screwed one way, the spirals seem to move in opposite fashion. So the elegance of Goethe's model is its complementarity. In the Introduction we said that a sign reorders time and space 'in' a hypothetical dimension. Similarly, a good model reverses the apparent irreversibility of time's arrow by means of the stipulation that in order of desire the end precedes the means; the future state of the solution is imagined. Before working out this temporal problem with any completeness, we must consider some larger qualities of time in Chapter 3. But for now we see in the turning screw the continuous transformation of form as right-handed spirals seem to go over and under into their opposite, and the detritus of the experiment is brought back as evidence of progress before one has arrived at the solution. Space and time are reversed in a Class D model of discovery. Insides are brought out, and the future is anatomized. In the turning screw, the asymmetry of the hand as a cutting tool is complemented by the fittingness of the cupping ground as a combining tool. This model of Goethe's therefore is the very essence of betweenness: everything which exists can go over into its opposite.

CHAPTER 2

Two-Dimensional
Semiotics

Two-dimensional semiotics features the pictorial aspects of signs, tools, and models. It highlights the interplay between the figured image and the two-dimensional ground which hosts the image. Although sometimes ignored in reading pictorial signs or sometimes diminished in board games, the semiotic plane often imposes a visual grammar which itself organizes images into significant relationships, as a Mercator projection, for instance, imposes its own arithmetical distortion upon the depicted movement of a ship. And since any limited representation calls attention to transcendence, a two-dimensional plane substitutes for a ground of action to which its visual signals refer, as a cartographic grid is transformed into a sea upon which a ship's movement is depicted.

Visual Memory

The complementary relationship between a pictograph and its planar context therefore serves as a visual mnemonic, a semiotic datum, of where one has been and from which one plans to depart. Points of departure are implied movements. So in order to understand the inclusion or suppression of apparent movement, either mental or physical, in Class B and Class E instruments, let us first consider cave paintings, one of the earliest forms of pictorial mnemonic. Surely the most remarkable recent thesis is Bertram D. Lewin's idea that the cave paintings of Lascaux are the earliest recorded visual memories.[1] Regardless of individual interpretations about the paintings, the cave itself must have been known as an archives where images were preserved (p. 37). Because each image is depicted as if it were a modern "still" extrapolated from animal motion, the "still" for Lewin is congruent with modern notions of memory "traces." Given that questionable identification of still and trace, he is able to conclude that the cave of Lascaux signified the head: "It was an externalized replica of the internal cephalic image, where our 'pictures' are stored and concealed. If this is so, the cave not only holds the earliest visual images but is also the first model of the memory and the mind" (p. 39). One might readily agree that the paintings in some way served as mnemonics of the anticipated hunt for the cave painters, and so it might be helpful for moderns to construe the cave as being an early model of mind, but it is unnecessary to retro-relate that idea of a cephalic model to the artists themselves. Although certainly self-conscious as human beings, the artists were not designing the source of their own mental images in the head, but rather were supplicating the absent animal by means of the remembered image. Although early Egyptian hieroglyphics similarly served as mnemonics and might serve as cephalic models for purposes of modern interpretation, nobody makes the mistake of maintaining that the Egyptian wall and its images were cephalic models for the Egyptain artists themselves.

For some anthropologists these Paleolithic visual mnemonics reinforced future action because they were symbolic plans. For instance, according to Rudolph E. Heyman, they were early versions of technical drawing.[2] He theorizes that a technical drawing is a systematized graphic representation of a three-dimensional structure. As such it plays down optic aspects in favor of a "haptic-kinesthetic component." In order to test his thesis he asks two people to draw a previously unseen object; one is asked to draw what he sees, while the other is blindfolded and is asked to draw with one hand an object he feels in the other hand. The person who sees the object will draw it "naturalistically," by instilling the illusion of depth. However, the representation of the feeling hand will lack "the habitual symptoms of three dimensionality," but will include "simultaneous different views of the same object." The result will be similar to abstract art and also to technical drawing: ". . . the only difference is that in a technical drawing the simultaneous views are put in agreed order" (p. 374). Cave paintings, for Heyman, were designed singly for practical purposes by people who gave primacy to a haptic-kinesthetic component, because by handling the objects of the hunt, by making and using implements, they were put in closer touch with animals than by seeing them naturalistically.

One can regroup cave paintings as objects of esthetic enjoyment, or perhaps as self-conscious attempts to see oneself processing a visual trace, or perhaps as technical drawings. Without ignoring the attraction of any of those groups, we shall regroup them as visual mnemonics designed for the anticipated-and-remembered practice of hunting animals. In that grouping, each pictograph is a member of Class B instruments, while the containing cave which includes all the pictographs is a Class E instrument. The pictograph of a bison is a practical sign that torques away from the planar wall in favor of humped lineaments, even to the degree of appropriating natural swellings and indentations in the cave wall. The pictograph suppresses movement, like a "still," by stylizing legs to such a degree that they are often merely suggested instead of being drawn naturalistically. The cave wall, however, cannot be seen in its entirety; one must maneuver through difficult passages with a torchlight. Both maker and viewer must follow a labyrinthine path that itself determines the sequences of images to be seen. Hence, one suddenly sees flashes of images that are then held simultaneously in the memory, while moving on to other groups of pictographs that describe situations which are similarly held in simultaneity in the memory and on the walls. That purposive movement with regard to visual signs is a process of storage and retrieval of infomation which characterizes Class E instruments. Although they highlight 2D and suppress 3D, they torque 1D in significant ways. We shall itemize these ways later in the chapter. For now, we construe the cave wall to be the field of action; its material component of clay or rock is ignored in favor of its abstract quality as screen, and the maker's and viewer's movement is torqued into the setting so that succession in the pictures is determined by walking the path. Although the wall holds the images in manifold, they are experienced serially.

Paleolithic cave printings may therefore be retro-related to the ancient rhetorical tradition of using architectural mnemonics to help oneself remember the sequence of a speech. The tradition of spatializing mental processes in architectural mnemonics is surveyed by Frances Yates.[3] She traces its use from classical Greece through Roman rhetoric to Renaissance theatre. The better to remember, according to this tradition, one chooses a well-known house, palace, or temple of some size and suitable diversity; then following a previously fixed route through the building, the mental traveler places, one at a time, a series of visual images—that coincide with significant passages of the speech—in featured locations throughout the building. Then while the orator is delivering a speech, he imagines himself walking through the building and retrieving each of the stored images along the way. That path of disclosure becomes his narrative, and the visual signs are the clues to Ariadne's thread strung through the labyrinthine sacred space of memory. Because the signs and buildings (Class B and E instruments) are constructed in no material medium, they serve as elements of a kind of thought experiment which is purely 'in' the hypothetical dimension, not having been depicted anywhere. Later in the chapter we shall return to this phenomenon, but for now it is necessary to define more precisely some different kinds of visual signs.

Hieroglyphs et al.

The visual signs of the cave paintings and the visual signs of the memory theatre depend upon different uses of abstraction. In *Visual Thinking,* Rudolf Arnheim defines "pictures" as images which "portray things located at a lower level of abstractness than they are themselves."[4] "Pictures" are those images which are more stylized than the object depicted, such as a picture of a bison. On the other hand, a "symbol" for Arnheim is a visual image which portrays things that are "at a lower level of abstractness than is the symbol itself" (p. 138). So in an architectural mnemonic a visual sign would not symbolize a real bird, but rather a transitional idea in a speech; the image of the bird might be retrieved in order to remind oneself that the next lead-in is to be the bird of the soul which flies out of the mouths of dying persons. While retaining Arnheim's useful distinction about different referents of abstraction, let us use the more traditional terms of pictograph and ideograph, because the term 'symbol' will be retained for Peirce's definition of a linguistic sign in Chapter 3. A pictograph is to be thought of as a visual sign which represents objects; an ideograph is a visual sign that does not represent objects but rather ideas. A pictograph is more 'abstract' than its object because it is dimensionally reduced. An ideograph such as the soul-bird uses two-dimensional aspects to depict an abstraction.

In both cases "Less is More," but in the first case abstraction is a means, while in the latter, an ideograph, abstraction is the end. Neglecting to discriminate between these two kinds of visual signs can lead to confusion about modeling discoveries. Consider, for instance, the famous case of the square circle as an apparent visual sign. On the one hand, the image can be drawn as a pictograph, where a circle touching equal sides of a square might represent a vertical view of a dome and its foundation walls. On the other hand, as an ideograph, the drawn image could represent a Renaissance ideal of geometrical proportion, as in Leonardo da Vinci's well-known depiction of the human figure with outstretched limbs touching the circle at equiangular points. But here P. W. Bridgman disposes with the image and thus with the whole idea of "non-being":

> We cannot say that such a thing as a square circle, for example, does not "exist" without implying by the mere fact that we are using the words and talking about "it" that a square circle has a certain kind of existence. What kind of existence this may be has provided philosophy with a topic for discussion for thousands of years. The quandary presented by this situation we can see is one which naturally arises in Indo-European languages—it would be interesting to know whether it is felt as a quandary in other types of language. It seems to me that the situation can be adequately dealt with by reducing it to the purely formal level. If we say, "The combination of words 'square circle' has no referent either in the objective external world or in the conceptual world of logically consistent objects," it seems to me that we have said all we need to say. I do not see why philosophers are not willing to say this and dismiss the topic from serious consideration.[5]

This is a practical point that Hobbes expressed earlier. But the discussion suppresses the long history of efforts to square the circle at the same time that it depends upon that history of frustration for the empty results of the task. It is the historical context of proven failure that yields the outcome of meaninglessness, not simply the illogical yoking (called "catachresis") of opposing linguistic symbols. On the contrary, it is the diachrony of effort by philosophers and mathematicians that allows the square circle to be scaffolded as a visual sign on the "purely formal level." Although the square circle is formally a placebo, it is not merely the extreme of a ritualized sign. (Must one similarly dismiss the Roman Pantheon whose dome when looked at vertically is an architectural embodiment of the square circle?) It is part of the humanistic record of hope, effort, and failure that is crucial for the liberal arts and the history of science to retain if one is to understand the problematic grandeur of discovery. Karl R. Popper calls this kind of history a "tradition of critical discussion," where conjecture invites refutation, and where failure is as important as success for the outcome.[6]

An understanding of that diachronic record is necessary if one is to value what I. J. Gelb calls "the revolutionary importance" of the phonetization of the visual sign.[7] Without an understanding of the history of hieroglyphic writing, its possibilities and its limitations, one cannot evaluate the shift from two-dimensional pictographs and ideographs to one-dimensional sounds that occur in time more prominently than in space. This process of further abstraction and displacement, where sounds are substituted for pictures, might belong more properly in Chapter 3; but it would be unwise to exclude temporal elements from the discussion of visual signs, because the invention of rebus writing can be correlated with a new attitude toward time itself. Rather than being a mythic pattern of seasonal repetition, time apparently began to be conceived then as something we thought to be peculiarly modern, once it was construed to consist of discrete and unique elements in some kind of linear succession. For example, rebus writing identifies drawn objects with other word sounds: draw a bee and a leaf for "belief." This new form of writing began simultaneously with the desire to represent a specific, unique event, such as a particular battle rather than a hieroglyphic picture which would simply signify "war" in general. Place names were added; then in the first dynasty visual signs of persons were depicted, plus their own names and titles (pp. 73–74). These annotations expressed unique events that were therefore discriminated from the events of forebears. They monumentalized individuals, by offsetting death. The discovery of time sprang from a desire to transcend its limitations. And rebic signs served well since they seemed to freeze process by converting fleeting sounds into spatial pictures. Egypt's monumental and funereal culture therefore evolved a semiotic ratio peculiar to its needs: Self-awareness is to death awareness as the construction of a unique rebus is to an individual's monument.

That very metaphysical conjecture about Egyptian picture writings should be counterbalanced by a different diachronic record, the practical needs of political economy as being the originator of Sumerian writing:

> With the rise in productivity of the country, resulting from state-controlled canalization and irrigation systems, the accumulated agricultural surplus made its way to the depots and granaries of the cities, necessitating keeping accounts of goods coming to the cities, as well as of manufactured products leaving the cities for the country (Gelb, p. 62).

The crucial difference between Egyptian wall writing and Sumerian record keeping is that clay tablets allowed the symbolic space of the visual sign to move literally through real space, as records accompanied the exchange of commodities.

This orchestration of moving and handling visual signs led to a revolutionary shift in the dimensionality of trade tokens, according to a recent theory about the origin of writing. Denise Schmandt-Besserat has explained that writing may have evolved in four stages.[8] About 10,500 years ago in the Middle East, three-dimensional tokens were used to represent different kinds of commodities as well as different numbers. She has correlated Sumerian cuneiform signs of ca. 3000 B.C. with many of these geometrical clay shapes that are about 5,000 years older (see Figure 13). For example, a drawn circle with a cross represents a sheep in Sumerian; it coincides with a similar three-dimensional token, an incised disc. Oil is depicted as a half circle connected to a triangle; its correlative is a tear-shaped three-dimensional

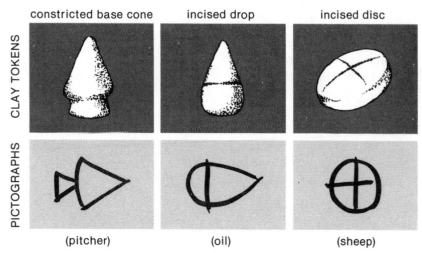

FIG. 13. Sketches of Warka clay tokens and picto-
graphs. Adapted from Denise Schmandt-Besserate,
"An Archaic Recording System and the Origin of
Writing," *Syro-Mesopotamian Studies.*

object with a line cut around the broad end. There are similar
correspondences with numbers.

The first stage in the evolution of writing may have involved
a middleman carrying these three-dimensional tokens inside a
sealed pouch from sender to receiver; so three-dimensional tokens signifying ten sheep provided a measure of accountability
when the items were delivered. The second stage occurred about
5,500 years ago when the geometrical shapes were put inside
hollow clay spheres called "bullae," and the sender's personal
seal was inscribed on its outside. In the third stage, the innards
of the bullae were duplicated on the outside by inscriptions,
when each token was impressed on the outer surface. The fourth
stage involved the understanding that the three-dimensional
sphere and its three-dimensional contents were no longer necessary: recording had become writing. In our terms, a two-dimensional plane became the ground, and the two-dimensional figures
were inscribed with a stylus. An architectonic instrument that
once had been handled was transformed into a two-dimensional

text that one read. This is an elegant example of ritualization, a principle of parsimony in the diachronic record, that shows an evolution from handling with three dimensions toward writing in two dimensions. But even at the last stage, the extreme of parsimony, a formal placebo, is counterbalanced by redundancy through duplication, so that meaning is not lost through least effort.

The development in trade of more sophisticated methods of transport, through intermediaries, proceeded hand in hand with the development of more economical forms of accounting and writing. For the exchange of items to ever more distant markets is paralleled by transformations in writing that are characterized by increasing relative distance between signifier and its original three-dimensional referent. The shift, for instance, from a pictographic method of representation to cuneiform writing, that is, where the abstract wedge-shapes of a stylus pressed in clay gave rise to a more abstract script, makes the relation between signifier and signified more difficult to discern. And once an arbitrary signifier like the letter *A* was agreed by convention to stand in the place of a spoken syllable rather than to depict a recognized natural image, the very notion of sympathetic relationships was suppressed. When a strict pictorial conection between signifier and signified was replaced by rote learning, then linguistic meaning shifted away from an image grounded in the natural world to an arbitrary hypothetical dimension reached by means of a logic based on the ability to wield abstract signs in alphabetical relations among themselves.

The "Flat" Field—
Theory of Mapping

Both ancient and modern authorities agree that far-traveling Phoenician traders were responsible for diffusing, if not for originating, the alphabet. They were practitioners of the distal signifier. In addition to that one-dimensional development they were present at the inception of mapping, an occupation where the two-dimensional plane came into its own. According to Greek geographers the first chart of the earth was drawn by Anaximander, kinsman of Thales, who apparently was of Phoenician extraction:

> Anaximander of Miletus, the pupil of Thales, was the first to depict the inhabited earth on a chart (ενπινακι γραψαι). After him, Hecataeus of Miletus, a much traveled man, made it more precise as to be a thing of wonder.[9]

The illustration (Figure 14) of Hecataeus' chart (517 B.C.) testifies to the "geometric spirit" at work in Anaximander's conception. On the one hand it seems based upon Thales' principle, discussed in Chapter 1, that the earth floats upon the sea, like a ship. But Karl R. Popper asserts that there is inherently an infinite regress in Thales' conjecture.[10] Anaximander's cosmology, however, did away with any notion of props or supports underlying the figure as a ground. According to Popper, Anaximander believed that the earth was like a cylinder or drum that is "held up by nothing, but remains stationary owing to the fact that it is equally distant from all things" (p. 138). For Popper, this conjecture about free suspension, as well as stability by means of equidistance, is all the more remarkable, because there is no analogy for it in the whole realm of observed fact. Its audacious thesis about equilibrium in a symmetrical system anticipates Newton's thesis about gravity. It recalls for us Thales' group of thinkers, the "Forever Sailors"; that idea of an eternal helmsman becomes the key to the self-regenerating principle of cybernetics, derived from the Greek 'helmsman'. The value of conceptual models, in this case a two-dimensional map, allows the possibility of thinking about the earth and its sun, moon, planets, and stars as a closed system and therefore as being governed by an internal principle of regulation.

FIG. 14. A reconstruction of Hecataeus' map of the world (517 B.C.). From *Ancient Times* by James Henry Breasted, © copyright Ginn and Company (Xerox Corporation).

Although there exists no explicit description of Anaximander's chart, it may have been less utilitarian and more like a conceptual model of the earth's structure. In Hecataeus' rendition, the earth still remains flat like a "disc," but Anaximander also constructed spherical celestial globes with concentric rings and radii inscribed on them that represent symmetrical distance, which would eventually become the method of dividing the earth in coordinates (Kahn, p. 89). By the time of Ptolemy, both latitudinal and longitudinal lines were described on flat planes of wood, clay, or brass that represented the earth.[11]

Horizons

From the time of the Phoenicians, movable charts and movable letters went hand in hand with the principles of economic transport. The power of extrapolation and of condensation in small-size planes can be realized when one recalls that the determination of latitude probably evolved from navigating via the Pole Star.[12] Vast distances on the sea can be determined from even vaster distances in space, if only one has a small visual mnemonic for guidance. By means of that mnemonic, navigators could determine their horizon by comparing it with angles off the Pole Star. This extrapolation of the horizontal plane, the x axis of the Cartesian grid, therefore evolved by looking up at it on the celestial sphere and by drawing it underneath oneself on the horizon of the earth.

This extrapolation seems so logical, so natural, that it comes as a surprise to think, with Raphael and with Giedion, that horizontality and verticality were Neolithic processes of abstraction. Paleolithic artists apparently did not orient their visual signs according to symmetrical horizons of straight lines running up and down or sideways. Theirs was a more manifold space. Their 'vertical' planes were topographical walls of caves, and their 'horizontal' planes were the natural topographies of horn and bone, upon which were encised visual signs. As J. Z. Young says of the same phenomenon, "Those who live in western-type houses and cities have an experience of vertical and horizontal lines that is different from an inhabitant of the jungle, who, it is said, does not experience the same spatial illusions. . . ." [13] The architectonics of the plumb line have imposed a conceptual grid that governs much of one's thinking about two-dimensional planes and their arrangement of visual signs.

But what of the observed horizon itself, that earliest of flat planes that the navigator extrapolated at sea? As he pivoted about his own vertical axis, like the leg of a compass, the sweep of his eyes and the curvature of the earth revealed a disclike horizon, a circular boundary. (See Figure 15, an illustration of a Babylonian map, where the point of the compass has been inserted to describe angle and hence arc.) It was observationally delimited but conceptually indefinite. "The outer limits of the earth's disc," depicted on Hecataeus' chart, extrapolates that observed phenomenon into an unobserved conjecture. In the experiential world, horizons divide what one sees from what he guesses about. Within that sensory horizon the nature of the world can be accordingly measured or verified in numerous ways. Henri Poincaré once said, "It is by logic that we prove but by intuition that we discover."[14] Beyond the perceptual horizon is the world of discovery: one of guesses, intuitions, and leaps to understanding. Now every two-dimensional plane, every two-dimensional model of discovery, uses finite lines that serve as horizons. A strange reversal of the theory of horizons occurs once one draws on a plane. If the horizon of a model is necessarily finite, limited by the hard boundary of a line, then two-dimensional models employ finite limits, with relations that can be measured or otherwise verified by logic, even though the symmetries and logics are really conceptual extrapolations of what one cannot see but what one guesses about, that is, what is indefinite and not necessarily limited to measure.

Descartes, for example, grappled with this problem when he tried to explain to Henry More his notion of the indefinite extension of matter:

> For it is God alone whom I understand possibly to be infinite; as for the others, such as the extension of the world, the number of parts into which matter is divisible, and so on, whether they are *simpliciter*

infinite or not, I confess not to know. I only know that I do not discern in them any end, and therefore in respect to me, I say they are indefinite. And though our mind is not the measure of things or of truth, it must, assuredly, be the measure of things that we affirm or deny.[15]

Fɪɢ. 15. Babylonian map of the world with indented compass point. Reproduced courtesy of the Trustees of the British Museum.

Alexander Koyré traces this aspect of Cartesian doubt to the earlier teaching of Nicholas of Cusa, for whom the universe is "in the full sense of the word, *indetermined.* It cannot, therefore, be the object of total and precise knowledge, but only that of a partial and conjectural one" (p. 8). This learned ignorance, for Koyré, is the first step in breaking the closed horizon of a finite universe.

Torsion on the Grid

The development of perspective in Renaissance painting and the rise of coordinate geometry are sometimes yoked together as one phenomenon; and to the extent that both methods bespeak a larger concern with systemization, the yoking has its rewards in the history of ideas.[16] Our concern will be to understand the phenomena as different kinds of exercises, since each method exploits separate advantages of the two-dimensional plane and its accompanying pictographic signs. Historically speaking, in the early fifteenth century, tracing contraptions consisting of a threaded net or grill (*graticola,* as Alberti termed it, Figure 16) were devised so that the pictorial image could be transferred piecemeal to a paper on which was inscribed a corresponding network.[17] So these perspective grids antedate Cartesian coordinates; in fact Descartes himself did not use a complete grid system. His followers devised the polar system of coordinates later in the seventeenth century. He himself worked only in what might be called the north-east quadrant described by the x-y axes.[18] The two-dimensional grid in painting was a device for fostering the illusion that one is looking *through* it, "like a transparent window," as Alberti said, "into a section of the visible world" (Panofsky, p. 603). But the polar coordinates in geometry were axes of relation that allow one to fix moving points *upon* the plane.

FIG. 16. Dürer's woodcut of nude and grid (c. 1527).

In other words, a Renaissance painting exploited the potential depth of the plane, of looking into the window so that one saw a receding landscape. By heightening the illusion of representing one space 'in depth', the Renaissance artist also fixed the scene in one time. The hock cart wending its way homeward full of the harvest, with a weary laborer plodding alongside, signifies by its arrested details and its slant of light on autumn afternoons a precise instant of time as well as of three-dimensional space. Mannerist paintings, however, such as Salviati's "Bathsheba Betaking Herself to David" (Figure 17) exploit simultaneous movement by refusing to let objects vanish into the background of the paintings:[19] "If the three-dimensional illusion of depth has proved to be a cul-de-sac of one time and one space, the two-dimensional features many spaces in multileveled time."[20] A Cartesian grid is similar to this Mannerist painting. But the revolutionary nature of Descartes' thinking was its practicality. He combined two hitherto dissimilar disciplines, algebra and geometry. By associating algebraic equations with geometric curves and surfaces, Descartes created "one of the richest and most fruitful veins of thought ever struck in mathematics."[21] By conceiving a pair of numbers that were to be thought of as locating a unique point on the x-y grid, Descartes and his followers could therefore chart on the grid the arc of a cannonball or the movement of a

FIG. 17. Salviati, *Bathsheba Betaking Herself to David.* The torsion of her body reflects the complementary forces of anticipation and reluctance. Gabinetto Fotografico Nazionale, Rome.

ship. And by locating several points on the curve, one could apply temporal increments to the values, whether Bathsheba or ship. The possibility of locating simultaneous views of an object in systematic order upon a two-dimensional plane is Heyman's definition of "technical drawing," as explained in his theory of cave paintings.

With the emergence of perspective and with the rise of coordinate geometry, the structuring of torsion upon the two-dimensional plane came into its own. The two-dimensional structure of Class B and Class E instruments was used to mathematicize art and to regularize nature into symmetries of geometrical curves. Class B instruments highlight two-dimensional, torque three-dimensional, and suppress one-dimensional aspects. This class appropriates the transparency of the visual sign so that one looks through the medium of paint into the illusory depths of the plane, where the vanishing point is achieved by the obliquity of perception. Time is frozen into a fixed instant, and is therefore suppressed. In Class E instruments, however, two-dimensionality is highlighted, one-dimensionality is torqued, and three-dimensionality is suppressed. The illusion of depth is sacrificed for the surface value of the plane; on it one can depict simultaneously the successive instants of a curved path. In Class E instruments the possibilities of the memory theatre have been used to their fullest potentiality, by depicting all at once the various transitional points to be used, while doing away with three-dimensional architectonics. Put another way, Class B instruments use the torqued phenomena of perception, where, for instance, a mosaic floor pattern of hexagonal discs is stretched and diminished, to achieve the obliquity of depth through the painted plane. But Class E instruments use torsion as a means to draw attention to movement-in-time as an integral. Salviati's Bathsheba reminds one that paintings may belong to Class E. And Cartesian grids may belong to Class B, when a third axis (z) is added to x and y; then one looks through the plane into an oblique space that becomes less Euclidean and more hypothetical as one adds algebraic points that no longer subscribe to the limits of three space.[22] Neither of these classes is inherently superior to the other; each has its limitations that are defined by the complementarity of space and time. For instance, in a Renaissance painting, the cul-de-sac of one time and one space is known as a cul-de-sac only by virtue of the synchronic view of a Class E painting—a Persian miniature, for instance, where different scenes are stacked simultaneously on top of one another. That is, in a Class B painting where time is suppressed, its very suppression of time into a frozen instant may call attention to diachrony. And in a Class E painting the synchronic conversion of four Bathshebas will call attention to spatial distortion. In this case, David's assignation is not with a seraglio, but with one woman who is pulled two ways in a diachrony of reluctance and anticipation.

Contorting the Plane

Coordinate geometry takes its rise from utilitarian efforts to locate signifiers algebraically in a curve upon a plane. But neither that exercise not the three-dimensional obliquity of depth in a perspectivist painting exhausts the possibilities of torqueing two-dimensional instruments. What is the semiotic function of warped coordinates, where the grid itself is curved or in some other way redesigned? That is a topological question, for topology is "the geometry of distortion. It deals with fundamental geometrical properties that are unaffected when we stretch, twist or otherwise change an object's size and shape."[23] Since the real world does not have the elegant symmetry of Euclidean fictions, topology seeks to understand those properties of the real world which remain invariant when objects are skewed.

As a separate discipline, topology traces one of its beginnings to a famous formula expressed by the Swiss mathematician,

Leonard Euler.[24] In any simple polyhedron, the relationship between its vertices (V), its edges (E), and its faces (F) may be formulated as

$$V-E+F=2$$

Richard Courant and Herbert Robbins prove this formula by asking the reader to imagine that any simple polyhedron is hollow and is made of thin rubber. Cut out one of the faces; then stretch out the remaining surfaces until they resolve themselves into a plane. We shall not continue the proof of that formula. Instead, we can observe with Panofsky that Dürer's "proto-topological" method of projecting polyhedra on a plane (Figure 18) allows a similar reconstruction back to three space (p. 619). The proof of Euler's formula and Dürer's network depends upon the capacity of the plane to be folded or otherwise transformed.

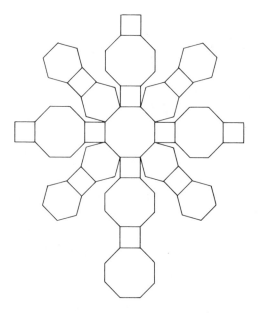

FIG. 18. Dürer's net of the *Cuboctahedron Truncum*, from his *Unterweisung der Messung* (1532).

In some primitive art a similar process involves the transition from three-dimensional constructs to two-dimensional representations. Here Boas describes the making of a bracelet:

> The animal is imagined cut in two from head to tail, so that the two halves cohere only at the tip of the nose and at the tip of the tail. The hand is put through the hole and the animal now surrounds the wrist. . . . We have thus recognized that the representations of animals on dishes and bracelets must not be considered as perspectivist views, but as representing complete animals more or less distorted or split. The transition from a bracelet to the painting or carving of animals on a flat surface is not a difficult one. The same principle is adhered to. . . . [25]

Boas speaks of the 'unfolding' of an animal; it therefore achieves a kind of 'orthogonal projection' similar to Dürer's and Euler's planar representations. These two-dimensional representations are interpreted or deciphered, therefore, by a metaphorical process of reassemblage back into three space; the simultaneous depiction of bilaterally symmetrical aspects of the animal allows the plane to be remodeled. This can be tested by actually cutting out a Haida figure depicted on a page; then by a process similar to the Japanese art of *origami,* one can fold the figure into three-dimensional symmetries.

In the Renaissance the painting plane was also distorted by a perspectivist trick that has come to be called "anamorphoses."[26] Panofsky here translates Galileo, who argues that both allegory and anamorphic art distort nature wrongfully because in those modes nature must be seen "obliquely"; whereas he claimed that one should "accommodate" oneself to nature and not vice versa. These trick pictures, for Galileo, "show a human figure when looked at sideways and from a uniquely determined point of view but, when observed frontally as we naturally and normally do with other pictures, display nothing but a welter of lines and colors from which we can make out, if we try hard, semblances of rivers, bare beaches, clouds or strange chimerical shapes" (p. 13). According to Panofsky the most famous example of anamorphic art is Holbein's "Ambassadors" (Figure 19): "A strange, chimerical shape" inhabiting the foreground resolves itself into a death's head, when viewed from the extreme lower left and from underneath the frame. As a visual pun it conflicts with the pomp of ambassadorial splendor. As a coded signature, it may also celebrate the artist: 'hollow bone' depicts a rebic translation of Holbein.

Galileo's 'frontal' bias may have contributed to his failure in adapting his own circular view of planetary motion to Kepler's ellipse. In any case, the understanding that two-dimensional planes can be proto-topologically encoded has been widely used in modern efforts to understand the way that the environmental grounds of nature can shape figures by adaptation. Perhaps the most well-known illustrations (Figure 20) of this phenomenon are D'Arcy Wentworth Thompson's morphological distortions of different families of animals within a species.[27] His "oblique" coordinates graphically signify both the invariance and the transformations in figure-ground complementarities. These Class E models are not visual puns. The method of wrenching Cartesian coordinates provides a way of graphically depicting pervasive and therefore unrecognized contexts that may be shaping the adaptations of significant figures. When Wittgenstein said, ". . . treat of the network and not of what the network describes," he gave proper prominence to the planar grid, but insufficient attention to the complementary figures that result from distorting the network.[28]

Thompson's Class E models are 'ideographic' because the forces that wrench the coordinates cannot actually be seen in real space but only in the hypothetical dimension that is illustrated. For another example, consider Bertrand Russell's extremely 'graphic' thought experiment for imagining the abstraction known as relativity.[29] You are in a balloon suspended over a night landscape observing a large beacon at the top of an increasingly

FIG. 19. Hans Holbein the Younger, *The Ambassadors.*
To discover the skull raise the lower level of the picture to eye level; then tilt the picture back to the right
along your line of sight. National Gallery, London.

steep hill. Because it is very dark, you do not realize that the
beacon is on a hill. Nor do you see men carrying lanterns over
paths in a varying topography of smaller hills and vales. Because
you see only the lanterns and the beacon, you assume that the

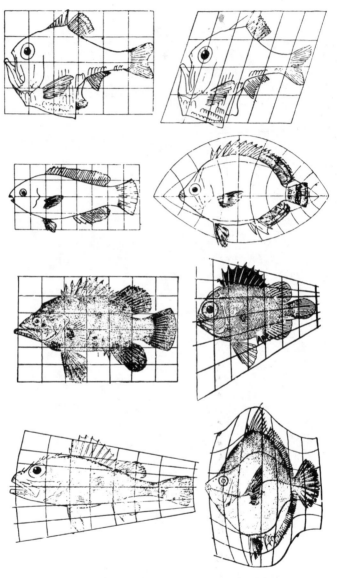

FIG. 20. Modulations of fish on distorted grids. From D'Arcy Wentworth Thomson, *On Growth and Form.* Cambridge University Press.

large flare is exerting influence upon the smaller ones. That situation is analogous to the Newtonian idea that the sun exerts influence at a distance upon the courses of the other planetary bodies. At the dawn, however, corresponding to the new light of Einstein, you see the hills, and you realize then that the beacon itself has nothing to do with gravity. The wandering bodies are really following topographical paths of least effort, whose angles increase as the hills become steeper in that neighborhood of space-time. Russell advises the reader "not to try to picture this [hill in space-time], because it is impossible." And yet in preparation of this analogy, Russell had asked his reader to sketch coordinates on an India-rubber ball and then to twist the ball so that the coordinates will vary (pp. 73–74). Hence topology is described as "rubber-sheet geometry." This kind of topological sketch (Figure 21) has become known as an "embedding diagram."[30] The visual thinking of Russell's landscape is so vivid that one might be convinced he is observing a Guy Fawkes celebration with Eustacia Vye on Thomas Hardy's Egdon Heath. In other words, an analogy can become so refulgent that its visual properties may improperly substitute for phenomena that cannot be observed. Hence the advantage of the embedding diagram, which is almost as abstract as the abstraction to which it refers.

Advantages and Limitations of Classes B and E

Visual representations upon planes belong to a category of signs that C. S. Peirce called "icons."[31] Icons are mainly distinguished by their pictographic qualities. The signifier stands for the signified by resemblance between the picture of a fox and the animal depicted. Peirce isolated two subclasses of icons that he called "images" and "diagrams." For example, representational signs of a fox's image, the sleekly narrow head, the bushy tail, and the

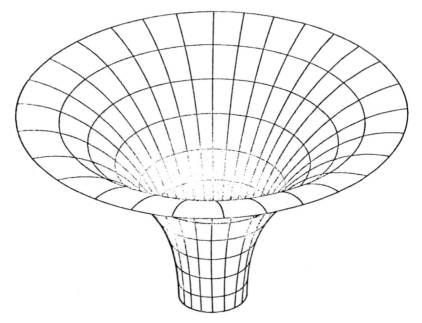

FIG. 21. An embedding diagram sketched to suggest
the curvature of space in the neighborhood of a massive object. From Kip S. Thorne, "The Search for
Black Holes," *Scientific American.*

supple outline crouched to the earth are sufficient to make the
remembered connection with that animal. In diagrams, however,
the likeness is achieved "only in respect to the relations of their
parts" (p. 107). A diagram is "an icon of relations and is aided
to be so by conventions" (p. 107). Although the algebraic signs
that help one to plot positions upon a Cartesian grid are not
iconic, the relations that they express about the signified qualities
are iconic. Hence for Peirce any algebraic formula is primarily
iconic; for us, any embedding diagram also depicts an iconic
relation. This distinction between icon and diagram reinforces
the differences between Class B and Class E semiotics; the former
is primarily 'naturalistic', though it can be extremely stylized,

while the latter includes technical drawing, topological grids, and other planar constructions that measure relations.

A similar way of highlighting the different qualities of these classes is James J. Gibson's distinction between the "visual field" and the "visual world."[32] The first is the world that one sees; the second is the world that one knows. In the visual field one scans in saccades, one focuses, one adjusts to parallax. In the visual world of conceptions one adjusts the visual field into known constants, such as the conventions of Newton and Euclid. To rephrase the situation in Peircean terms, one constructs what we have called Class E instruments in order to see diagrammatically those known but unperceived relations of the visual world.

E. H. Gombrich maintains that a visual image lacks precision when unaided by language or by other norms of past experience.[33] Because pictures without captions allow a wide range of possibilities, their capacity for extra coding is rich. For instance, a favorite motif in Chinese decorative art is a group known as the Three Friends: pine, bamboo, and plum. According to story, the motif arose during the Yuan or Mongol dynasty. These hardy perennials were able to withstand the cold winds from the north; so the pattern encodes a passive resistance to the Mongol invaders.

In Oriental art it is understood that nature can be rendered intelligible only by way of conventions, but all too often one collapses those conventions into nature itself: Once a master was commissioned to paint a forest of bamboo. When the patron saw that the masterpiece was painted entirely in red, he ventured to object that it was unnatural. The master said, "In what color should it have been painted?" "In black, of course," replied the patron. "And who," said the artist, "ever saw a black-leaved bamboo?" Visual images, like human utterances at large, point to an end beyond themselves, but the executed imagery can be so arousing, can attract so much attention to itself, that its conventions are mistaken for nature.

On the other hand, Rudolf Arnheim argues that visual thinking has a kind of graphic clarity which langue cannot approach. "Purely verbal thinking is the prototype of thoughtless thinking, the automatic recourse to connections retrieved from storage."[34] Arnheim says that there are two kinds of visual thinking, intuitive and intellectual cognition. The categories correspond to Gibson's. For intuition involves scanning the perceptual field of a painting, while intellectual thinking consists of systematically isolating and identifying "the numerous components and relations of which the work consists" (p. 234). Arnheim illustrates the difference with a group of three men (p. 235), depicted here in Figure 22. By scanning the situation one almost immediately intuits the comparative sizes of the stick figures. But if one were not given the illustration but rather were presented with these propositions,

A is taller than B
B is taller than C
Therefore, A is taller than C

then the comparative sizes must be carefully elaborated, for two self-contained instances must be combined in order to derive a third instance. This chainlike series of linear propositions is therefore overrated in terms of precision. But when the two types of thinking are combined, they grace one another. The near simultaneity of the pictorial image is then complemented by the step-by-step modification of the intellectual process.

The relative size of the three figures is determined by an assumption that they exist on a flat plane as do Class E instruments, rather than in a vanishing point where figures B and C are 'really' the same size as A but are farther in the background. A sufficient rejoinder would be that, since no illusion of the third dimension is sketched into the background, a *gestalt* need for

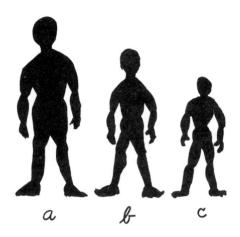

FIG. 22. Drawing of three men showing the power of visual thinking over the circumlocution of language. From Rudolf Arnheim, *Visual Thinking.* University of California Press.

simplest form demands that one see the whole as a diagram. However, that principle of parsimony is tacitly reinforced by invisible vertical and horizontal lines that enclose the figures. It may be that post-Cartesian Westerners cannot avoid seeing any illustration as existing on a grid; that is, binary opposition may be a constant of our "visual world."[35] However that may be, the metaphor of warp and woof, derived from the two-dimensional designs of weaving, preoccupies this culture, because the products of the loom are so basic to it.

The metaphor of warp and woof allows a bilateral view of reality. Consider that a vertical slice of the world can be cut in order to build a wall or a longitude. Both are constructed vertically but viewed horizontally. Then, too, a horizontal slice allows one to look vertically, up at the stars or down at a point of sailing. A child in the fifth grade must 'grasp' that simple paradox if he is to understand the meridians on a map.

Because metaphors are linguistic models, these examples of warp and woof should be more properly included under the chapter about one-dimensional semiotics. They are therefore appended as epigraphs to this chapter as nets that skein two-dimensional design:

1: These two modes of apprehending structure are the warp and woof of our experience. Pictures, blueprints, most diagrams, chemical structural formulae, are state descriptions. Recipes, differential equations, equations for chemical reactions are process descriptions. The former characterize the world as sensed; they provide the criteria for identifying objects, thereby modeling the objects themselves. The latter characterize the world as acted upon; they provide the means for producing or generating objects having the desired characteristics. —Herbert A. Simon, "The Architecture of Complexity"

2: History is a tissue made of fate and achievement; on one side the garment shows only its warp, but if it is turned we may notice only the woof. —Bruno Snell, *The Discovery of the Mind*

3: Still, all the while like warp and woof, mechanism and teleology are interwoven together, and we must not cleave to the one nor despise the other; for their union is rooted in the very nature of totality. —D. W. Thompson, *On Growth and Form*

4: This warp seemed necessity; and here, thought I, with my own hand I ply my own shuttle and weave my own destiny into these inalterable threads. Meanwhile, Queequeg's impulsive, indifferent sword, sometimes hitting the woof slantingly, or crookedly or strongly, or weakly, as the case might be; and by this difference in the concluding blow producing a corresponding contrast in the final aspect of the completed fabric; this savage's sword, thought I, which finally shapes and fashions both warp and woof; this easy, indifferent sword must be chance—aye, chance, free will, and necessity—no wise incompatible—all interweavingly working together. —Herman Melville, *Moby Dick*

The pervasiveness of warp-and-woof metaphors testifies to human fascination with "Polar Analysis," as F. Vaihinger called it.[36] In Chapter 4 we shall review further the polar perspective as it combines synchronic and diachronic axes. But when used in metaphoric discourse as above, the real usefulness of the grid has been bypassed in favor of the pictorial vividness of the method. When the grid is transposed from a Class E instrument to a different class (in this case, Class F), the intent is not to literalize the mechanics of warp and woof, but rather to 'depict' by implication the complementary workings of large design. When ordinary language is insufficient to describe a conjecture, then one usually 'accommodates' a parallel mode of discourse in order to extend the horizons of description. Similes that use "like" or "as" draw attention to parallelism; however, metaphors transgress parallelism in favor of a new category that includes two hitherto unconnected categories of use. Metaphor is an intentional "category mistake." In lapsed metaphors, such as "I see the light!", the figurative element has disappeared through over-use. But this kind of linguistic discussion must await Chapter 3.

CHAPTER 3

One-Dimensional Semiotics

The signifier, being auditory, is unfolded solely in time from which it gets the following characteristics: (a) it represents a span, and (b) the span is measurable in a single dimension; it is a line.

Saussure,
Course in General Linguistics

In the preceding chapter the figure-ground relationship between the image and its plane was stressed. And in the first chapter there was featured the relationship of the three-dimensional object instrumentally extending from the hand toward a hypothetical ground. Now the relation between the linguistic sign and the unidimensional line will be set forth. One-dimensional semiotics is more abstract than the other classes: first, because it suppresses the kinesthetic thingliness, the materiality, of 3D objects; second, because it suppresses or transforms pictorial qualities on a plane; third, because it calls attention to time, a difficult concept to 'grasp' since it has no adequately abiding explanation except by way of movement; and, finally, it is more abstract because 1D semiotics achieves the precision of numerically pure ratios.

Class C and F Signs in Time

In accord with the figure-ground organization of previous chapters, signs are laid out here as abstract figures that operate together in a chainlike sequence, a diachronic ground. As a visual mnemonic for this mode consider briefly the tradition of retrograde writing, or *boustrophedon,* which meant 'ox-turning' to the Greeks because one read in the same direction as the plow turned.[1] A number of linguistic figures formed and read together form a sequentially patterned ground. For example, the form of writing called 'cursive' literally means 'running'. The figures were connected one to another by a swift hand that could keep pen to papyrus as much as possible.

As with previous classes, Class C includes the figural aspect, and Class F includes the significant ground of the discourse. Class C highlights a 1D aspect, while torquing 2D and suppressing a 3D aspect. Class F highlights a 1D aspect, while torquing 3D and suppressing a 2D aspect. Class C examples, such as the letter A, the number 1, the note C#, are units of discourse read as 2D images on a page that have been atomistically extracted from time; but Class F examples, such as a poem, a sonata, a chemical equation, are acted out in sequence, accomplished in motion, and understood in time. Class C abstract figures are bits extrapolated from process; when they are set in operation, they successively comprise a sequential ground of discourse, a Class F construct. Because a Class F construct exists only in the time when it is being read, recited or performed, its beginning-to-its-end, its duration, is enacted in clock time, but also in a hypothetically temporal dimension that is apart from mechanical chronology. That duration is a part of psychological time, where attention span is paramount; when one is bored the clock moves slowly, and vice versa. As with Class D models, where the symbolic material may be confused with matter, so in Class F instruments the enacted time may be confused with clock time. Although measurable with the same instruments, their quality is different. For with an enacted beginning-to-end, a Class F instrument has a separate temporal mode that appears to give it a separate harmonic structure, a three-dimensional torsion, a sacred space, that is similar to but distinct from ordinary experience.

Perhaps the most important distinction to be made between the temporality of clock time and the duration of unidimensional semiosis is one that springs from the apparent irreversibility of time's arrow.[2] For many philosophers, mathematicians, and physicists, time must be subordinated to spatial considerations, because time is but a figment of consciousness that can ultimately be measured only by the expansion of the universe.[3] Having "no objective physical significance," time is a bugbear that causes much disagreement about its interpretation:

> But time has important characteristics that clearly distinguish it from space. Apart from its one-dimensional nature, the two principal features peculiar to our conception of time are its arrow and its passage. Whereas time's arrow depicts the irreversible before-and-after succession of events, time's passage refers to the distinction that we make between past, present, and future. These two closely related properties must not be confused.[4]

It is important for this study that those temporal properties of consciousness be distinguished, because the definition of the linguistic sign, and indeed the issue of discovery itself in the several dimensions, all ride upon the distinction that the future is of an order different from the succession of events into before and after. As we shall see, to say that time is unidirectional is not to say that the future is hidden in the present. Furthermore, to say that time's arrow cannot be reversed is not the same as saying that the past cannot be retrieved semiotically, for we can repeat psalms, recipes, experiments. For instance, we can reenact *Oedipus Rex,* a play explicitly about the theory of fictions, for it enacts the conversion of time's arrow and reversibility. The magic of symbolic repetition, as Oedipus retracks through history the murderer of the King of Thebes, is subsequently undermined by his tragic awareness that he cannot reverse the order of events as they actually occurred. In other words, we must replay Oedipus semiotically so as to be forewarned that while cultural history parallels heredity—the sequence of parents and children—the history of culture can be reinterpreted, but it cannot modify genetic history as it once happened for all time.

But how does the future enter? One-dimensional signs are strung together in chains of linear order that work contextually in semantic and syntactic blocks of timed release. One-dimensionality might seem to be the very epitome of thought processes, since consciousness is, first of all, one's consciousness of before and after. But as Whitrow says, thought of succession is different from succession in thought, for in thinking retrospectively about a sequence, one necessarily holds it simultaneously.[5] Hence mentation is not simply a one-dimensional mode, but almost necessarily involves a meta-situation, wherein simultaneity, the absence of succession, is involved. The concept of simultaneity, however, is heady, for its inclusiveness might seem to allow for the chaining of the future into a lockstep with past and present. In that regard, the world is like a film strip, as William James explained, a "block universe," where all the photographs are 'already' there and are being run by for our experience.[6]

The essential reason why the future must be understood as being a different order of experience is really a semiotic phenomenon: the need to forge linguistic signs is part and parcel of a need to explore, to intervene, with that which has not yet come about. That is a need different in kind from the not-yet-divulged state of a block universe. In Chapter 1 we noticed, with Young, that the very emergence of *homo sapiens* is yoked with the ability to plan, to make tools for potential use in an anticipation of the future. The linguistic sign is a special case of tool making, for as Peirce explained, its very being is future oriented: a 'symbol', for Peirce, refers to a general class of things:

Thus the mode of being of the symbol is different from that of the icon and from that of the index. An icon has such being as belongs to past experience. It exists only as an image in the mind. An index has the being of present experience. [It is physically associated with an object, as smoke is coterminous with fire, or as fever is the index of disease.] The being of a symbol consists in the real fact that something surely will be experienced if certain conditions are satisfied. Namely it will influence the thought and conduct of its interpreter. Every word is a symbol. Every sentence is a symbol. Every book is a symbol. . . . The value of a symbol is that it serves to make thought rational and enables us to predict the future.

Whatever is truly general refers to the indefinite future, for the past contains only a certain collection of such cases that have occurred. The past is actual fact. But a general law cannot be fully realized. It is potentiality; and its mode of being is *esse in futuro.*[7]

In order to isolate the conditional nature of the future and its relation to the linguistic sign, the symbol, let us set Peirce's statement against one of Whitrow's about the future:

> *The past is the determined, the present is the moment of 'becoming' when events become determined and the future* is the as-yet *undetermined.*
>
> There is indeed a profound connection between the reality of time and the existence of an incalculable element in the universe. Strict causality would mean that the consequences pre-exist in the premises. But, if the future history of the universe pre-exists logically in the present, why is it not already present? If, for the strict determinist, the future is merely "the hidden present," whence comes the illusion of temporal succession? The fact of transition and 'becoming' impels us to recognize the existence of indeterminism and irreducible contingency in the universe. The future is hidden from us—not in the present, but in the future. Time is the mediator between the possible and the actual.[8]

Whitrow here italicizes the high point of his thesis about time and the future. His shares with Peirce's passage the potential act that begins to define the incalculable element beyond one's ken. In this sense, to know is to recognize the boundaries of one's ken. For our purposes, therefore, we shall define the future as a temporalized version of the hypothetical dimension. It is an arena that the linguistic symbol probes in order to make manifest the ideas for which one gropes. Better than any other dimensional instrument, linguistic signs serve to define, but not necessarily to discover, what Michael Polanyi calls an "emergence," a higher law, like Peirce's, that is unspecifiable, even in terms of the particular linguistic units that launch it.[9]

Questions about 'general' or 'higher' laws immediately invoke the question of logical types, with which we opened this study. Since potentiality cannot be bound, except by linguistic symbols which are open ended themselves, it is necessary to make manifest the idea that not only symbols such as "anticipation" are open ended but that all symbols, in their reference to a general class, are contingent. It is in this sense that Eco defines a sign as involving "a process of unlimited semiosis."[10]

If linguistic signs are temporally oriented toward the future, are they therefore not of the past; or are icons strictly of the past? Clearly not so. Just as Peirce was careful to maintain that icons, indices, and symbols all utilize the possibilities of the others, so we stressed in Chapter 2 that visual mnemonics, though associated with the past as memories of it, are oriented, like any other tool, toward future needs. One remembers in order to predict. One of the earliest mnemonic analogies in Western literature, Plato's aviary from the dialog *Theaetetus,* was imagined in order to serve as an example of what we would call storage plus retrieval of information:

> . . . let us suppose that every mind contains a kind of aviary stocked with birds of every sort, some in flocks apart from the rest, some in small groups, and some solitary, flying in any direction among them all. When we are babies we must suppose this receptacle empty, and take the birds to stand for pieces of knowledge. Whenever a person acquires any piece of knowledge and shuts it up in his enclosure, we

must say that he has learnt or discovered the thing of which this is the knowledge, and that is what 'knowing' means.

Now think of him hunting once more for any piece of knowledge that he wants, catching and holding it, and letting it go again.[11]

Although this lovely analogy concerns a Platonic complex of learning (remembering, forgetting, reselecting), the several linguistic symbols (Class C) create such a vivid image that one tends to think of the bits of knowledge as pictographic icons instead of as abstractions. In other words, symbols may partake of iconic qualities as they are needed, and icons may be preserved in architectural mnemonics so that they may be retrieved for future purposes.

"In the order of desire or intention, the end, according to St. Thomas, comes before that which is done toward the end."[12] Although the future has not yet been accomplished, in the order of desire it precedes the several kinds of instruments that are potential means to effect that end. That is why models in any hypothetical dimension precede their eventual solution. They temporalize the hypothetical dimension by enjoining the future to become actual. While any model contingently preempts the future, only unidimensional writing can articulate with precision the relations betwixt past, present, and future. And the English language—despite its Whorfian detractors who might celebrate an inflected language that decategorizes tenses into less arbitrary boundaries than Past, Present, Future—is nonetheless remarkably explicit in temporal demarcation.[13] For Whitehead, those inflected languages such as Latin or Greek "express an unanalysed complex of ideas by the mere modification of a word; whereas in English, for example, we use prepositions and auxiliary verbs to drag into the open the whole bundle of ideas involved."[14] As Lyons observes, *deixis* (Greek for 'pointing') is a linguistic term that refers to the orientational features of language, specifically with regard to space and time (pp. 275, 304).

As a deictic category, a hypothetical dimension in the future may be conjectured with precision by language and by writing.

One-dimensional Landmarks

Since our study involves only those symbolic instruments that artificially preserve, in another medium, thought and language which defer time's eventual effacement, we shall not devote attention to the ways that number words are spoken or to the ways that some cultures count on their fingers. Although important in a cultural history of numbers, those methods vanish once they are enacted; whereas Karl Menninger shows that long-lasting tally sticks were "universal" mnemonics among early cultures.[15] Everywhere that Menninger looked among early cultures, he found wood to be the "paper" of the common people, and knives and styluses to be their "pens," and grooves or notches their "letters" (p. 224). The materials and methods of this form of accounting remain in many European words for the exercise of writing. Perhaps the most important example is the word 'book'; it "takes its name from the *Buche* or 'beech wood' from which the wooden writing tablets were originally fashioned, just as the Latin *liber* is named after the 'bark' and the Greek *biblos* after the papyrus, on which it was written. The material on which the writing was done thus gave its name to the written product" (p. 225). In numerous cultures the wooden tablets were tied together at one end in bundles or stacks, so that they took the semblance of a book as we know it.

Furthermore, the very word that Peirce used to denote the linguistic sign, 'symbol', is part of a more sophisticated development in the cultural history of the tally stick, according to Menninger. In many countries, tallies served as contracts between two people, each of whom retained half of a broken tally as a check of security: "A *check* is thus an 'identification mark,' just as the Greek word *symbolon* originally meant a 'distinctive mark' (Greek *sym-ballein,* 'to throw together')—that is, a broken shard, for the most part with writing on it, which fitted the piece from which it had been broken" (p. 233).

The simplest form of tally stick represents an order of succession without the need for numbers as we know them. Menninger observes that it is a mistake to believe that a tribe having only number words up to 'three' cannot count beyond that number (p. 34). By matching a notch with any object, a significant group can be arranged. Whether it be cows or sheep, whatever, the principle of order is possible because of the abstract quality of the notches, which have no intrinsic character, only a relationship with others in the same series of notches. A tally notch is therefore the most rudimentary symbol, at the same time that it is most abstract, when one abstraction fleetingly is monumentalized into an object.

Surely the most remarkable conjecture about unidimensional ordering is Alexander Marshack's thesis that Paleolithic people etched time by tally sticks.[16] Marshack insists that all cultures are in different ways "time factored," that the inevitability of temporal succession creates in humans an urgency to account for change in time. The revolutionary inclusiveness of his thesis is its application to an extremely large number of Paleolithic engraved bones that hitherto had seemed to be geometrical in their notchings but meaningless in their specific use. Marshack argues that they are lunar calendars, that as early as 30,000 B.C. our Ice-Age ancestors were annotating successions of nights by changes in the semblance of the moon. Three-dimensional objects were not being counted; rather, time itself was being kept. For Marshack, humans are not so much tool makers; indeed, "man the tool maker" is a coinage of the post-Darwinian era, where, economically speaking, the fittest tool makers survived to make the best culture (pp. 62–63). Instead humans are characterized by their capacity for "thinking in time." Human brains allow "the processes of preparation, search and research, recognition, comparison, analysis, and deduction. . . . It is this time-factored, time-factoring, and visual-kinesthetic cognitive ability that is the human basis for science . . . (p. 67). Put another way, humans can work in and with several semiotic dimensions, but they must always work in time and with an accounting of time.

Especially in Paleolithic hunting cultures, where seasonal migrations succeeded or failed by time, the tallies of lunar cycles nevertheless suppress all specific occasions of passing time. Although as mnemonics they might serve to predict the timing of impending events—such as migrations, pregnancies, hunts, and the like—still the signs themselves (the Class C instruments) were pure abstractions of succession. Each slash or dot was a stark indicator of a passed temporal unit. For example, since a human gestation period is completed within the span of ten moons, the specific number of days need not be crucial if the counter can group ten significant sets that would correspond to ten fingers. We have already spoken of the hands drawn on cave walls, but many hands have missing fingers. Perhaps they were not amputated as signs of propitiation, as has been assumed, for they could be finger counting. A hand with no fingers would immobilize a hunter, but its representation might mean *five,* as it does in other finger-counting cultures. Be that as it may, the consistent grouping of ten units can be understood without either the number *ten* or without a finger 'language'.

The consistent grouping of signs according to lunar phases is not directed toward number itself but toward a periodic pattern of lunar waxing and waning represented by slashes or dots. Time is not so much the issue as timing, the proper point within a process to act. When "Readiness is all," unidimensional signs serve as measurements that connect recollection and anticipation, what is passing and to come. Those very abstract slashes, therefore, hinge the past and the future into an apparent unity;

hence linguistic symbols largely contribute to the fallacy that the future is of an order identical to the past and to the present.

It has been said that the intuition of mathematics begins with the abstraction of 'twoness' from all specific occasions in time: "Mathematics arises when the subject of twoness, which results from the passage of time, is abstracted from all specific occurrences. The remaining empty form [the relation of n to $n+1$] of the common content of all these twonesses becomes the original intuition of mathematics and repeated unlimitedly creates new mathematical subjects."[17] Whitehead put it a bit differently in *Science and the Modern World:* "The number 'two,' for example, is in some sense exempt from the flux of time and the necessity of position in space. Yet it is involved in the real world."[18] That explains Whitehead's position with regard to the Pythagorean faith that mathematical entities were the forms out of which all other constructs follow in the world.

Marshack's tally slashes are not signs of arithmetic extrapolated from time. They are emptied of specific content, however. The mathematics of twoness, emptied of specific occurrences, serves in this case as a special case: all linguistic signs are general laws extrapolated from specifics. Symbols, or unidimensional signs, are like mathematicians themselves, as Einstein wrote to Mrs. Born, "completely insubstantial."[19]

The Pythagorean mistake, as we shall see, is the first mistake of 1D semiotics: to compound linguistic signs with the stuff to which they are applied. Although these lunar tallies are emptied of particular events in time, most early civilizations infested their calendrical symbols with the causes of temporal succession. Semiotics and kinematics were confused. That is, signs themselves were not only thought to be descriptive, as were the markers at Stonehenge, but were thought to be prescriptive, as were the characters in the Mayan calendar. How did this combination arise? Signs can be construed as simple mnemonics designed to forestall forgetfulness in time. For signs arranged in systematic order, both linguistic and mathematical, are static images set in a serial code that divides and classifies the flux of duration into a significant pattern. Hence the illusion can arise that fleetingness has been arrested by the magical relationship among signs. There occurs a conflation of real time into symbolic time, as the symbolic messengers of change are confused with the agents of causation. For example, in many ancient cultures the taboos accorded the messenger and the herald were assigned in order to drive a distinction between the bearer and the cause of bad tidings. In calendrical lore, a simple principle of reflection symmetry is at work to cause the confusion: instead of the sign being a deictic pointer that marks a point in the transit of moon or sun—such as a carefully located dolmen—the sign could be construed as mirroring the control of time passing. By means of a mirror reversal, the sign becomes a model of astronomical power, itself directing humans to act at an opportune time. In our terms, a Class C sign has been confused with a Class F sign; an arbitrary annotation has been confused with an imitative model of time.

Ratios

In the beginnings of number signs, there was a similar semiotic confusion between what Hogben calls "flock numbers" as averse to "field numbers."[20] In flock numbering, the meaning of the total *fifty* is invariant, though the signified varies with need, whether with cattle or sheep, whatever the flock or group. However, in field numbering, where size and shape are concerned and where there is an a priori measuring device such as an acre, the meaning of the numeral *50* varies with the magnitude of the measuring device. Especially in measuring areas, the numerals do not seem to be completely insubstantial. And we must recall that number figures were not even used in actual calculation by the ancients. Calculations were done on an abacus; numbers were used only to record the results of calculations. Doing sums and other arithmetical figuring had to await the zero. We shall presently return to these distinctions, for the Pythagoreans used dots to represent numbers.

One of the most useful discoveries, if not the most important, in the history of unidimensional semiotic has been Newton's universal law of gravitation. Not so well known is Newton's further effort to explain the nature of gravity to his own private satisfaction. In so doing, he had to weed through ages of semiotic conflation about ratio. In his unpublished writings as well as in accounts of his contemporaries, there is ample evidence that Newton believed the Pythagoreans had worked out the inverse-square law before him in their theory of chords as applied to the music of the spheres.[21] How was it that Newton would embroil himself with that most notorious sect of number magicians, for whom number was the secret of the universe and harmony their god? Despite their notoriety as number philosophers, their famous theorem has been the most fruitful law for subsequent physical discoveries in and about the universe. Despite the fact that the law—the sum of the squares on the two shorter sides of a right-angled triangle is equal to the square on the side opposite the right angle—is only true for small surfaces, yet its eminence as a ratio is explained by Russell: ". . . everything in geometry, and subsequently in physics, has been derived from it by successive generalizations. The latest of these generalizations is the general theory of relativity."[22] Russell's explanation of the track from Pythagoras, through Descartes, through Newton, through Gauss, to Einstein, is a bellwether of narrative clarity; and for those who might need to review Newton's inverse-square law, Russell's chapter "Intervals in Space-Time" might be a good place to begin. The important distinction for our purposes is Russell's thesis that although interval is common to all those physical and geometrical discoveries, interval has different values as ratio, much like field numbering. To put it another way, most subsequent universal laws have treated Pythagoras' as a special case. Recognizing those similarities, Newton retro-related his law into the mysteries.

By comparing his law with Pythagorean laws of chords, we can explore a fascinating example of semiotic conflation, where the Pythagorean law of chords is not treated as a special case, but where it subsumes all subsequent variations as special cases of its universality. As we shall see, the semiotic problem is one of understanding the mathematical problem of numerical ratios as well as the iconic problem of relations and how they differ.

According to some historians, the Pythagorean theorem was probably derived from a useful mnemonic of Babylonian astrologers and/or Egyptian surveyors: knot a rope at twelve equidistant intervals; lay the rope taut on the ground, and form an angle at the end of the third knot; then count four more knots and form another angle. The remaining five knots, when stretched back upon the original angle, become the hypotenuse of a right triangle. The Egyptian land surveyors were known as "rope stretchers."[23] Pythagoras' brilliant generalization loosed them from the progression 3–4–5 at the same time that it proved the progression:

$$3^2+4^2=5^2$$
$$9+16=25$$

Once the Egyptian recipe of 3–4–5 was understood, any length could be set on the ground, using any set of interval on the cord. It was therefore the emergence of a ratio of intervals that was all important, not the specific length of the intervals on the rope.

Now let us conjecture that as the surveyors of acreage and the builders of temples stretched their ropes on the ground, they must have become handy with degrees of tautness along the rope just as they were privy to different values of field numbers given to the unifying ratio of 3–4–5. As they stretched and plucked the rope for uniform tautness, their ears might have detected a characteristic pitch at three, four, or five knots, where the knots correspond to nodes of frequency on a plucked string. Apparently it was an early Babylonian discovery that the pitch of notes is partially determined by the length of the string. The three-dimensional mnemonic of 3–4–5 knotted intervals therefore could not only be used by the Pythagoreans as a visual point of departure for the all-inclusive formula ($Base^2 + Perpendicular^2 = Hypotenuse^2$), but it could also be used as an auditory ratio for extrapolating harmonic values.

Sometime during the sixth century B.C., the somewhat mythical Pythagoras discovered that the octave is in the ratio of 2:1, and the fifth of 3:2, and the fourth of 4:3.[24] That is, a particularly harmonious sound is formed by plucking two equally taut strings, with one twice as long as the other. "In our language, the interval between the two notes is an octave."[25] Again, the interval can be expressed by number, but the number does not refer to specific lengths but to relative proportion, to scale. The *tetractys*, the sacred Pythagorean symbol for the number 10, was a symmetrical composite of the first four integers (Figure 23). The symbol was musically significant for them because it "furnished the basic consonances of octave, double octave, twelfth, fifth, and fourth (2:1, 4:1, 3:1, 3:2, and 4:3)."[26] Laid on its side and stretched into a right-angled triangle, their symbol—but let us call it an icon— looks more graphic (Figure 24). Although conceptually helpful in displaying the numerical ratios involved, the *tetractys* in Figure 24 is iconically misleading with regard to the relative length of the string. For the single string is marked in the tetractys by one dot; whereas it is the longest of the series, being unencumbered by a node. When a node is placed midway along that string, then it plays an octave higher. The ratio of two to one is displayed, but the two dots mean that the string has been halved.

Perhaps to think once again about the 3–4–5 knotted rope in this context would make the intervals appear more graphic. The rope stretched out and unknotted would be unity, or one.

Fig. 23. The Greek *Tetracytys,* an important geometrical configuration of the first four numbers.

(The vibration with the lowest frequency is called the "fundamental" in music theory.) Divided in half and plucked, the octave sounds harmonious with unity. Then divide the unity one-third along the way, as in Figure 25, letting the knots represent nodes and vibrations.[27] In Figure 25 the first part of the series depicts the node placed one-third of the way along, so there are three numerically equal vibrations. The string plays a fifth above the octave, and the relation is 3:2. Place the node one-quarter of the way along, and it then vibrates a fourth, an octave higher, where the ratio is 4:3. Finally, if the node is fingered one-fifth of the way along, the harmonious sound is a major third above, but apparently the Pythagoreans did not reach that stage in the progression. Hence our icon is merely a graphic reconstruction and cannot be homologous with a step in Pythagorean thinking. Or else one can assume, with Newton, that this last step, much like his own law, was hidden from those uninitiated who were not privy to the secret order of the mysteries. In any case, the sketch shows why Newton would be intrigued by the intervals and their ratios. For just as the pitch rises as the length of the string is lessened, so the frequency of vibrations increases as length decreases. Frequency, in other words, is inversely proportional to length.

However, our iconic conjecture of Figure 25 is iconically misleading with regard to the frequencies depicted. The 3–4–5 knotted rope depends upon equidistance between knots; so while

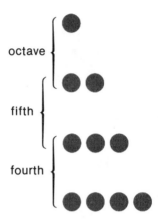

FIG. 24. *Tretractys* reoriented to show harmonic relations.

each of the three parts of the rope that form the legs of the triangle are successively lengthened, the intervals between the knots remain equal. But the harmonic progression depends upon a string or strings of equal length, and the frequencies or intervals between nodes become shorter or longer as the string is lengthened or shortened. In Figure 26, the frequencies increase in number and they decrease in length (and width) as the string is shortened. Although Figure 25 fails to be iconically accurate with regard to sound frequencies, perhaps its inaccuracy points to a Newtonian conflation. For neither he nor the Pythagoreans were able to measure frequencies in time, nor were they able to photograph a vibrating string. In the absence of temporal accuracy, Newton may have assumed that the musical intervals were of equal length because they were equidistant in an individual series. The physical distances of the inverse-square law depend upon equal intervals for the solution of the formula, but harmonics uses equal strings to achieve greater and lesser intervals. The conflation of Figure 25 involved semiotic confusion with ratios themselves.

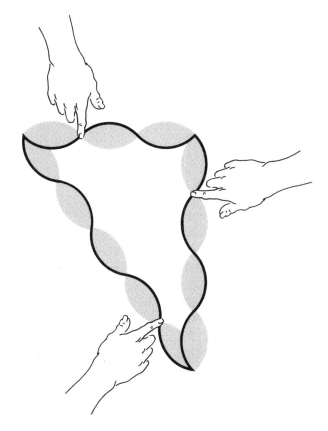

FIG. 25. Defective hypothesis about 3–4–5 harmonics.

When the Pythagoreans were able to reduce music to simple mathematical ratios, they were unable to limit their discoveries to string harmonics, but thought in addition that they perceived the same intervals in wind and bell ensembles, as well as in cosmic harmony.[28] Needham argues that the Chinese also made the same mistake, at least with regard to bell harmonics, at about the same time.[29] It was this application, or misapplication, of musical harmony to cosmic law which convinced Newton, as we shall see,

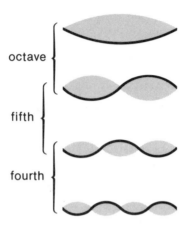

FIG. 26. Sketch of harmonic frequencies.

that the Pythagoreans had worked out the law of gravitation earlier than he had. Newton's law expresses the idea that two objects attract one another in proportion to the product of their masses and in inverse proportion to the square of their distance:

$$\text{Force} = \frac{Mm}{r^2}$$

In one of his later manuscripts, Newton "asserted unequivocally," as McGuire and Rattansi say, that the Pythagoreans understood the inverse-square law with respect to strings, and that they extended the ratio to planetary weight and motion.[30] For Newton, Apollo's lyre of seven strings was an ancient symbol of godlike harmony that stood for the relation of the sun to the remaining six planets, where the "intervals of the spheres [were measured by] the intervals of tones." It is this identification of two different kinds of "interval"—one a numerical ratio of sound frequencies and the other a numerical ratio of physical distance —that fascinated Newton:

But by this symbol [of Apollo's lyre] they indicated that the Sun by his own force acts upon the planets in that harmonic ratio of distances by which the force of tensions acts upon strings of different lengths, that is reciprocally in the duplicate ratio of distances. For the force by which the same tension acts on the same string of different lengths is reciprocally as the square of the length of the string.

The same tension upon a string half as long acts four times as powerfully, for it generates the Octave, and the Octave is produced by a force four times as great. For if a string of given length stretched by a given weight produces a given tone, the same tension upon a string thrice as short acts nine times as much. For it produces the twelfth, and a string which stretched by a given weight produces a given tone needs to be stretched nine times as much weight so as to produce the twelfth. And, in general terms, if two strings equal in thickness are stretched by weights appended, these strings will be in unison when the weights are reciprocally as the square of the lengths of the strings. Now this argument is subtle, yet became known to the ancients. For Pythagoras, as Macrobious avows, stretched the intestines of sheep or the sinews of oxen by attaching various weights, and from this learned the ratio of the celestial harmony. Therefore, by means of such experiments he ascertained that the weights by which all tones on equal strings . . . were reciprocally as the square of the length of the string by which the musical instrument emits the same tones. But the proportion discovered by these experiments, on the evidence of Macrobius, he applied to the heavens and consequently by comparing those weights with the weights of the Planets and the lengths of the strings with the distances of the Planets, he understood by means of the harmony of the heavens that the weights of the Planets towards the Sun were reciprocally as the squares of their distances from the Sun (p. 117).

What Newton means in our terms is that if two objects are at a certain distance apart at one point, and if they are twice the distance next time they are measured, then their mutual gravity will be one quarter of what it was when first measured, or the inverse square of the distance. As one of his followers expressed it, according to McGuire and Rattansi, "A musical chord gives the same notes as one double in length, while the tension or force with which the latter is stretched is quadruple: and the gravity of a planet is quadruple of the gravity of a planet at double distance" (p. 117).

If the Pythagoreans understood the inverse-square law, of action at a distance, why then did they not proclaim it abroad instead of using their idea of celestial music caused by the rubbing together of solid crystal orbs? McGuire and Rattansi cite Newton himself: "Philosophers so loved to mitigate their mystical discourses that in the presense of the vulgar they foolishly propounded vulgar matters for the sake of ridicule, and hid the truth beneath discourses of this kind" (p. 117). So they substituted a system of bell harmonics of "solid orbs" striking one another "as though a greater sphere emitted a heavier tone as happens when iron hammers are smitten." In the remainder of the superb essay, McGuire and Rattansi depict a Newton discontented with the stance of the objective scientist who disdained to explain gravity in any terms other than the empirical mechanics of measurement and induction. The Newton of the unpublished manuscripts is a product of Cambridge Platonism, a Renaissance philosopher trying to uncover, not so much discover, old truths understood by the ancients but lost in time. The point is that Newton was not content simply with the numerical ratio of his universal law of gravitation, revolutionary as it was. He also sought the meaning of gravity as a relation expressing God's Harmony. For Newton, Apollo's lyre encoded the cosmic relations, and the Pythagorean ratio of chords provided the mathematical formula. In Gregory's *Elements* the ratio is explained, "whereby equal Tensions act upon Strings of different Lengths (being equal in other respects) are reciprocally as the Square of the Lengths of the Strings." In order to make that formula abide with his own, Newton needed to add only the product of two bodies' mass; hence the two kinds of discordant ratios were brought into unity.

We have said that the importance of the 3–4–5 knotted rope was the awareness that the numerical ratio stands independent both of the specific length and of the specific measure, whether inch, foot, or yard, to use familiar terms of measure. For Newton's contemporaries, of course, the splendor of his law, his elegant ratio, was its independence of different kinds of matter. No matter what class of material was being measured, it worked for small particles or for cosmic bodies. The law was universal because it could measure the attraction between any two kinds of matter, without paying heed to other herds or flocks that it might otherwise have belonged to. (The new class of materialism therefore emerged.) But the result of the formula being worked out with regard to two or more masses of matter at certain distances yielded a field number. If, for example, the field number were 50 pounds per square inch, but we wanted to convert to feet, the result would be one twelfth of 50. So in this regard the signifier '50' varies in inverse proportion to the new units of measure, but the actual ratio between the two signified masses remains constant, regardless of how it is expressed. Perhaps Newton himself initially conflated this kind of semiotic reciprocity in believing that his inverse-square law was hidden in the icon of Apollo's lyre, wherein the sun god, Apollo, who was also the god of music, governed the planets by way of harmonics. The weights and tension imposed on strings and the masses of cosmic bodies are two different classes of matter, which exhibit constant ratios and which semiotically vary according to field numbering inversions. Despite these variations on a theme, string harmonics and cosmic bodies remained distinct; Newton did not finally state that harmony is a cosmic law.

Another distinction remains to be made between Newton's law and the Pythagoreans'. Plato said that "God always geometrizes." Geometry preserves in spatial mnemonics laws of form that Newton was content to phrase in a unidimensional mode of mathematics. Although he was fascinated by the iconic relations

'in' Apollo's lyre, and by what it seemed to preserve geometrically, he nevertheless did not construct any such geometrical
figure, perhaps because he saw that without a unidimensional
written text a geometrical figure is subject to variant interpretations. On the other hand, except for the question of its historical
origin and except for its as yet undiscovered future uses, there
are no hermeneutic questions about the formula $B^2+P^2=H^2$. As
Russell shows, it was applied and reapplied with ever more significant variations until Einstein suggested that the temporal interval between events must be included with the spatial distance
between two points.

At this point, where temporality once again enters the question of unidimensional semiotics, we must heed P. W. Bridgman's
warning: ". . . it is meaningless to say literally that a velocity, for
instance, is equal to a length divided by a time. We cannot perform algebraic operations on physical lengths, just the same as
we can never divide anything by a physical time."[31] Algebra and
time are semiotic abstractions that perform operations in a hypothetical dimension called the mathematical formula; but since
they are of a logically different class, they cannot interpose literally upon physical events. Inverse-square semiotics expresses
variations on the abstractions—space, time, gravity—and while it
expresses crucial relations, it does not itself vary the actual ratios
between bodies. That distinction was best made by Whitehead,
who called it the "Fallacy of Misplaced Concreteness." Since the
distinction is important for one-dimensional semiotics, we shall
conclude the chapter with its discussion. And we shall pick up the
thread of inverse-square formulas in the conclusion to this book.

Spatialization of Thought

Perhaps thinking can be done intuitively without benefit of semiotic representation. If so, then one cannot prove the assertion,

though one may, in the absence of semiosis, trust. The process of thinking cannot be presented without distorting the process into some productlike thing. For the making and usage of semiotic objects, even symbols with individual substances abstracted contributes to an illusory sense of concreteness. When symbols are taken to be concrete, then the fallacy of misplaced concreteness has occurred. For Whitehead, seventeenth-century scientific materialism was most responsible for fostering the illusion.[32] The successes of Galileo and Newton in measuring matter in space and in time gave rise to the simple faith in those abstractions—space, time, and matter. Further, it gave rise to subject-object or subject-verb dualism that in turn gave rise to materialistic psychology like the Lockean, which emphasized those material manifestations of mind which could be measured deitically and which relegated "secondary qualities" of mind to the fictions of poets and philosophers.

But this orthodox scientific trust in simple deictic location is really an illusion of concreteness from the perspective of a quantum of action, in which matter, space, and time cannot be so confidently separated. Writing like Bridgman above, Whitehead maintains that time, for instance, is of a different logical category than space. Although both are deitic pointers, the function of time is different with regard to matter: "First, as regards time, if material has existed during any period, it has equally been in existence during any portion of that period. In other words, dividing the time does not divide the material. Secondly, in respect to space, dividing the volume does divide the material" (p. 49). Temporality, therefore, is an accident with respect to matter, not an essential, an assertion with which we opened.

The other part of this duality is Whitrow's assertion that consciousness or mind has no spatial locus but exists solely 'in' a temporal dimension. Although brain has mass and occupies space, mind is "essentially *temporal* in nature, like a tune"; it has no "spatial extension nor precise spatial location."[33] Depending upon the way that argument proceeds, it might involve the same fallacy by geometrizing mind into a formal sequence; that is, it could spatialize temporality unwittingly. But Whitrow elsewhere cites Locke, who is often a whipping boy in this kind of argument, in order to take a more modern position (p. 223). In a chapter of the *Essay* where Locke discusses time and space, he concludes: "expansion and duration do mutually embrace and comprehend each other; every part of space being in every part of duration, and every part of duration in every part of expansion." Given Locke's modernistic insight that space and time are merely words that perhaps too conveniently separate a continuum where there is no such distinction, we are enjoined to recall that temporality, indeed unidimensionality at large, is merely a significant extrapolation that isolates one perspective upon unity in order to highlight sequential relations. The spatialization of thought into words that seem more concrete, because they are more abiding than wordless intuition, and into words that simultaneously seem to be more abstract than other semiotic tokens, this spatialization of thought is a necessary evil that makes symbols seem both 'abstract' and 'concrete', words which are both powerfully suggestive, like 'space' and 'time' that are best thought of as convenient labels and not as inhering in the nature of things. The fusion of two logically different kinds of words, with respect to matter, into the phrase 'space-time' highlights a perspective toward interval and toward continuum that is better discussed in the next chapter about four-dimensional semiotics.

To conclude, the fallacy of misplaced concreteness provides a caveat against the simple location of any sign, tool, or model in a so-called physical dimension. It is especially appropriate to unidimensional semiotics, because the fleetingness of spoken syllables seems to be preserved in linearity when they are written as symbols. Mentation can not be encapsulated, even in 'time'.

CHAPTER 4

Four-Dimensional
Semiotics

Four-dimensional instruments include the three Euclidean dimensions, but, in addition, they explicitly include some aspect of motion that is measurable in time. They are Class D instruments, which highlight 3D, suppress 2D, and torque 1D. Hence, for our purposes, 4D implements are not constructions of non-Euclidean geometry, which allow their practitioners to ponder mathematical extrapolations of 4–5–6–7 . . . or n dimensions. Nor when we speak of the fourth dimension do we mean a hypothetical or conjectural dimension, for all semiotic instruments operate therein, not simply 4D units. Instead, four-dimensional implements are models of holism. They are efforts to duplicate whole systems in miniature. But miniaturization is a term of relative magnitude. The model may be as large as the recent one of the Chesapeake Bay that extends for fourteen acres. Even then, as with any model, the designers chose only those aspects of the system that were most crucial to their larger ecological project. They knew, as do all modelers, that a whole system is impossible to duplicate. For example, it is logically impossible to reproduce the exact double of a cat, because one would be unable to 'keep up' with its temporal regulations, such as genetic, metabolic, or nerval information. Three different increments of time pertain to those regulators: the usefulness of genes transcends the lifespan of the individual in preserving the species; hormones are released over a period of years within the individual; nerve cells work within spans of seconds so that the cat can respond immediately to changes within its environment.[1] Even 'whole systems' are therefore perspectivist, providing a selective aspect of the problem to be constructed.

'Field' History

This historical sketch is designed to highlight that revolutionary shift of the early twentieth century when many different disciplines embraced holism as an epistemology of discovery. Immediately, therefore, one must confront the objection that at least two of those disciplines, structural linguistics and Gestalt psychology, apparently excluded a temporal dimension from their consideration of whole structures. If the eighteenth century was the era when most disciplines became historicized, then some disciplines of the early twentieth century rejected that diachrony for a synchronic perspective. As Morton Bloomfield put it in a brief historical sketch of linguistics, "Modern linguistics began in 1786 when Sir William Jones suggested that Sanskrit, Greek, Latin, and possibly other languages had a common ancestry. The problem of the universality of language was suddenly historicized, as befitted the rise of the historical age."[2] The phrase "synchronic linguistics" was coined by Ferdinand de Saussure, who first distinguished its principles of study from "modern linguistics."[3] Saussure thought that all disciplines would profit by "indicating more precisely the co-ordinates along which their subject matter is aligned" (p. 78). In Figure 27, the axis AB, for Saussure, is the axis of simultaneities, "which stands for the relations of coexisting things and from which the intervention of time is excluded." CD is the axis of successions, the diachronic axis, "on which only one thing can be considered at a time but upon

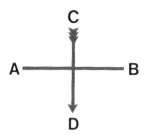

FIG. 27. Ferdinand de Saussure's coordinates, as sketched in *Course in General Linguistics.*

which are located all the things on the first axis together with their changes" (p. 80).

Saussure's relativistic perspective toward the spatio-temporal coordinates of language is nicely set forth in his analogy with a game of chess: "The respective value of the pieces depends on their position on the chessboard just as each linguistic term derives its value from its opposition to all other terms. In the second place, the system is always momentary; it varies from one position to the next" (p. 88). Each move of a piece systematically varies the synchronic axis, according to the unchanging rules of chess. "Rules that are agreed upon once and for all exist in language too; they are the constant principles of semiology." Semiology, for Saussure, is a general science of signs, generally synonymous with semiotics, of which linguistics is a special case (p. 16). Despite those preexisting conventions, each chess move has a "repercussion on the whole system," with variant significance depending upon the revolutionary nature of the move. Perhaps the most important part of the analogy is Saussure's claim that each move achieves an equilibrium that is conceptually different either from its antecedent or subsequent states. Furthermore, the route by which a state is reached makes no difference: "one who has followed the entire match has no advantage over the curious party who comes up at a critical moment to inspect the state of the game" (p. 89). For Saussure, in other words, the history of observed moves or modifications of the set has no necessary value in analyzing the state of meaningful oppositions at any point in time. The only real difference between chess and language, in Saussure's view, is that the latter achieves different synchronic states via fortuitous chance, such as unintentional vowel shifts, without the intentionality vested in the movement of chess pieces.

The elegance of Saussure's view—a horizontal slice taken across the evolving plant of linguistics, as he also expressed it metaphorically—was that the semantic sense of any one particular sign was seen as a product of its "relations" with all others in the set: ". . . everything is opposition" (p. 122), as figure is juxtaposed against the ground of discourse. After this thought experiment about simultaneity—and it is a thought experiment because one cannot *see* all the latent units of language that oppose and define one's selection and meaning of a word, though on can see all the pieces of a chess set—after this conjectural perspective, therefore, Saussure proceeds to discuss combination and selection, or "syntagmatic and associative relations." We shall not follow the rest of his theory, though we shall return later to the plant analogy.

In summary, the importance of Saussure's cross-sectional thought experiment was the revelation that each sign means nothing in itself; instead a sign demarks a difference in meaning from all other signs on the set: ". . . in language there are only differences *without positive terms.* Whether we take the signified or the signifier, language has neither ideas nor sounds that existed before the linguistic system, but only conceptual and phonic differences that have issued from the system" (p. 120, italics his). The revolutionary appeal of this insight, achieved by a horizontal slice, was sufficiently powerful to set aside the common-sense objection that words or terms must have inherent meaning. Its value for our purposes is that it now reveals the latent *ground* of language. Signs may be conjectured to be perspective units of "opposition," each of which contributes complementarily to the whole system of differences. For the first time, the *ground* of a semiotic system had been highlighted as a world of relations. Like Charles Darwin, Saussure was interested in the differences within a species.

Saussure was able to claim that his perspective downplayed temporal prominence because his own training and, indeed, his synchronic theory itself was derived from evolutionary linguistics. One who has played many chess games from beginning to end has an experience of diachrony from which to draw that the synchronic player lacks, who would analyze cross sections during the end game. It is not simply a pun to say that Saussure developed his theory of synchronic opposition out of an opposition to diachronic linguistics. As with literary study, in which the New Criticism emerged from historical criticism by way of learned men who were able to bring together a wealth of temporal context even as they analyzed the internal relations within an isolated work of art, so too could Saussure highlight synchrony while using diachrony tacitly. Hence, one must really recognize and use a complementary perspective, if only because in English, as well as in some other European languages, space cannot be discussed without invoking its opposite, time, and vice versa. But this limitation is not so much a failure of language as it is the understanding that any movement from state to state is not really a Newtonian abstraction of matter moving through empty space from point to point; that is Whitehead's prime example of misplaced concreteness. Instead, one must understand that movement or "motion is a relation," as Whitrow says.[4] Saussure's "relation" of linguistic signs within a synchronic state is therefore a special case of this other perspective upon diachronic relations. Compare Whitrow's description of "relations" with Saussure's:

> ... all our observations of distant events are associated with some time-lag. This means that *the world as observed at a given instant of*

individual time cannot be identified with the world as it is at a definite instant of universal time, for the more distant an object the greater the time-lag between it and the observer. Instead of seeing a succession of spatial states of the universe, we observe spatio-temporal cross sections (p. 183, italics his).

Saussure's synchronic cross sections therefore established an extremely useful kind of semiotic parallax, in which the shift of each linguistic sign simultaneously modified the relations of the whole field, but a 'modern' perspective toward space-time would seem to demand the consideration of temporal parallax as well.

To put Saussure in a historical context is to place his celebration of synchronic cross sections of the evolutionary tree within a movement that celebrates Einstein's presence. Roman Jakobson has shown how structural linguistics and relativity theory are historically similar, and perhaps even mutually influential.[5] Saussure's idea discussed above (although the rule governing a chess piece is invariant, the meaning of the piece emerges from the various transformations it undergoes at each subsequent place with respect to the other pieces of the set) was for Jakobson part of a larger European movement concerning topological invariance among *avant-garde* mathematicians and linguists of the 1870s. One of those theorists was the Swiss linguist Jost Winteler (1846–1929), whose principle of "configurational relativity" (*Relativität der Verhaltnisse*) was an idea ignored by his contemporaries, but perhaps employed by young Einstein. The boy lived with the Winteler family in Switzerland during the time of his famous thought experiment, and as an older man he always praised his "clairvoyant Papa Winteler."[6]

In still another discipline, Gestalt psychology, simultaneity and system were also stressed, though 'field' was the term used to describe elements of the former two terms. Since we have used the Gestalt terms 'figure' and 'ground' throughout in order to describe the semiotic relations of a sign, tool, or model, it is helpful to learn, contra Saussure, how spatio-temporal notions were transferred and modified from the discipline of physics. In Piaget's survey of structuralism he reports in the chapter "Psychological Structures" that Wolfgang Kohler had been trained originally as a physicist; "it was physics which suggested the notion, fundamental to him and to other Gestalt psycholgists, of the 'field'."[7] Just as we suggested in this Introduction, so Piaget leaves the impression that models are transferred from one discipline to another simply because the new model widens the horizons of discovery. But Kurt Koffka supplies a more human reason, one that helps to account for the widespread regard for holism in many disciplines during the early twentieth century: "One of the postulates of our psychology was that it be *scientific*" (italics his).[8] To the degree that theoreticians within a discipline desire to cloak their study with the rigors of science (and who is exempt from the wish for the most elegant ordering principles, even if they include noise, randomness, and indeterminacy?) to that degree will even remote disciplines become holistic, as if that very human wish would be assuaged by the impersonality of the 'field'. Even the arts, especially movements such as Cubism, were lured by scientism and concepts such as "field" painting.[9]

For Koffka and his colleagues Kohler and Max Wertheimer, the electromagnetic field had transformed the Newtonian world picture of "action at a distance," through the new physics of Faraday, Clerk Maxwell, and Einstein. Koffka summarizes their view in *Principles of Gestalt Psychology:*

Empty space as mere geometrical nothingness vanished from physics, being replaced by a definitely distributed system of strains and stresses, gravitational and electromagnetic, which determines the very geometry of space. And the distribution of strains and stresses in a given environment will determine what a body of a given constitution will do in that environment. Conversely, when we know the body and observe what it does in a certain environment, we can deduce the properties of the field in that environment. Thus we discover the magnetic field of the earth by observing the behaviour

of magnetic needles in different places, their declination and incli-
nation; similarly, we find out the gravitational field of the earth by
measuring the period of a pendulum of a given length in different
places (p. 42).

A tacit pun on bodies and environments allows the shift to psychological figures working within a ground or field of more or
less equilibrative forces, where psychological tensions are
equated with the stresses of physics. And the principle of self-
regulation, that maintains equilibrium for the organism, so
critical for four-dimensional models, is called by Kohler
"accommodation." It "means the creation of the best possible
conditions for clear organization" (Koffka, p. 311). For Piaget,
"self-regulation" is one of the several important properties of
structures;[10] hence our semiotics of accommodation must include organismic ideas of self-maintenance, through a cybernetics of anticipation and correction, or feedback.

In the field of biology this cycle of self-regulation was developed in the 1920s by Johannes von Uexküll, who termed it the
Funktionskreis, or functional circle, an elegant system of meshed
effectors and receptors that allows every organism to adapt to its
environment.[11] Ernst Cassirer transferred this circular system in
order to show that "symbols" intervene to help humans regulate
their lives in the same way. Just as animals regulate themselves
in their environment, so humans construct a "symbolic space" to
test the truth of propositions and judgments. In our terms, the
hypothetical dimension in which signs operate should be conceived as a loop of anticipation and correction.

According to Ludwig von Bertalanffy, the founder of "general system theory," the idea of organismic holism in biology
emerged from the mechanism-vitalism controversy; in his history
of whole systems, his own work appeared simultaneously with
Whitehead's theory of "organic mechanism."[12] But the idea of
'homeostasis' in biology dates back to the mid-nineteenth cen-

tury and the work of Claude Bernard, although the term belongs to W. B. Cannon. According to François Jacob, the biological principle of homeostasis for once provided a model that was transferred to physics, rather than the reverse: "systems observed in living beings were used by Wiener as a basis for the development of cybernetics."[13]

Trees in the Field

Almost as soon as the new physics of Newton arose, however, the idea of organicism emerged to combat the mechanical spirit. That is the main historical thesis of Whitehead's *Science and the Modern World*. Since 4D 'tree' models take their impetus from organismic assumptions, it will be useful to cite some early examples of organic metaphors, chiefly plants and trees. Like any other instrument, a metaphor becomes a model when it is systematically applied to the solution of an intimated problem, the intimation being that the model imitates in small the eventual configuration of the larger issue. But since most employers of organic metaphors were Romantic poets like William Wordsworth, who decried analytic system ("we murder to dissect"), the metaphors of organicism remained just that for most of them, metaphors and nothing further.[14] But when Goethe sought to be objectively observational, he kept a plant metaphor in his mind's eye. His 'primordial plant' (*Urpflanze*) ceases to be a rhetorical figure and becomes a model of discovery when it becomes both the object of his search and the means by which he would return to origination. As with the imaginations of so many other northern European artists before and since, his was seized by the exotic profusion of plants in the warm south of Italy:

> Seeing such a variety of new and renewed forms, my old fancy suddenly came back to mind: Among this multitude might I not

discover the Primal Plant? There certainly must be one. Otherwise, how could I recognize that this or that form *was* a plant if all were not built upon the same basic model?

I tried to discover how all these divergent forms differed from one another, and I always found that they were more alike than unlike. But when I applied my botanical nomenclature, I got along all right to begin with, but then I stuck, which annoyed without stimulating me. Gone were my fine poetic resolutions—the garden of Alcinous had vanished and a garden of the natural world had appeared in its stead. Why are we moderns so distracted, why do we let ouselves be challenged by problems which we can neither face nor solve![15]

As did the historical linguists following Sir William Jones, the Sanskrit scholar, Goethe began to ask evolutionist questions about form. In this Introduction we observed that his puzzlement about differentiated form rewarded him with the eventual insight that a sheep's skull is a fused extension of vertebrae. Stephen Jay Gould phrases the question about form in modern terms in a way that partially rectifies the quandary posed by Goethe: ". . . where did it [form] come from (a request for antecedent states in ontogeny and phylogeny), and what is it for? Although these questions are distinct in logic, we consider both when an analysis of antecedent states illuminates the function of a terminal product."[16] Gould is here addressing paleontologists, as well as those who are generally interested in the relations between ontogeny and phylogeny. The questions were also posed by comparative grammarians. In fact, Fredrich von Schlegel transferred the emerging principles of comparative anatomy to the pursuits of comparative linguistics.[17] A pupil of George Cuviers, the founder of comparative anatomy and a friend of Goethe's, Schlegel employed a biological analogy in explaining a proto-ethological investigation of linguistic differentiations in time: "Comparative grammar will give us entirely new information on the genealogy of language in exactly the same way in which comparative anatomy has thrown light upon natural history."

Searching for the earliest kind of tree model is similar to Goethe's search for the primordial plant, from which all subsequent forms evolved. Both are lost in antiquity, in cultural and in natural history, while the epistemological regress of things in time contributes to the fruitlessness of seeking absolute origins. Yet it is safe to assume with Ann Harleman Stewart that linguistic and physiological tree diagrams may be traced to the taxonomic and genealogical trees of medieval scholastics.[18] More important than the lost genesis of the type is Stewart's clear description of the genetic possibilities of the model itself, possibilities that certainly were part of Goethe's fascination with the forms of plants:

> The graphic elements of a tree diagram are the vertical and horizontal dimensions—given by the medium itself—and nodes and branches. Vertical and horizontal have, respectively, paradigmatic and syntagmatic import: things arranged along the vertical dimension are mutually exclusive; things arranged along the horizontal dimension are not. Thus the units on the vertical axis are those that do not occupy the same time or space; the units on the horizontal axis are not subject to this restriction. If the latter are defined negatively, this is because what they are not is more significant than what they are, in terms of the structure imposed on the data by the tree diagram; units on the horizontal dimension are defined by the fact that they do not participate in the mutual exclusivity which characterizes the vertical dimensions (pp. 13–14).

So far, there is no distinction between this tree diagram and Saussure's coordinates mentioned earlier. Where tree diagrams differ from Cartesian coordinates is in their further efflorescence into nodes and branches, where the combination of node and branch indicates "former unity" (p. 14), because the node depicts a time and space which 'later' was split into conditions equal to the number of its subsequent branches.

For Arthur Koestler, the advantages of a tree model are twofold: it displays hierarchic structure and it suggests an open rather than a closed system.[19] In Koestler's view of the tree as a model for a whole system, the diachronic and synchronic axes of other taxonomies are not imposed. Instead, it features the graphic display of a part-whole arrangement, or rather, a system of sub-assemblies, each of which is autonomous as it looks down the tree toward less complicated assemblies, but which is dependent as it looks up toward the several levels in the hierarchy (Figure 28). The advantage of this concept, which Koestler calls a "holon," is that it does away with misleading stumbling blocks such as atomism and holism or part-whole thinking habits (p. 197). At each level, therefore, a Januslike relativism exists between the constraints of rules generated by the next lower level and the next higher level. The "steady state" of each level, the "dynamic equilibrium," is achieved by the self-regulating codes of the open system, where each subassembly receives and sends information to and from the other levels. Even though there is no explicit inclusion of temporality in the tree model, still there is the dynamism of balanced forces, which is not a static state, but rather has the same kind of regulatory equilibrium of a fountain or a waterfall, as D'Arcy Thompson once explained the ceaseless flow of energy which configures a steady state.[20]

Just as a tree is not autonomous for Koestler, but may exist in relation to a forest, so there are interlocking hierarchies that are systematically related:

The trees are vertical structures. The meeting points of branches from neighboring trees form horizontal networks at several levels. Without the trees there could be no entwining, and no network. Without the network each tree would be isolated, and there would be no integration of functions. Arborization and reticulation seem to be complementary principles in the architecture of organisms. In symbolic universes of discourse, arborization is reflected in the "vertical" denotation (definition) of concepts, reticulation in their horizontal connotations in associative networks. This calls to mind Hyden's proposal that the same neuron, or population of neurons, may be a member of several functional "clubs" (p. 203).

A most inclusive icon of semiotic relations is here described as an organismic net extending through four dimensions.

Each level or cross section, for Koestler, is an "environment," and all creatures operate within a "hierarchy of environ-

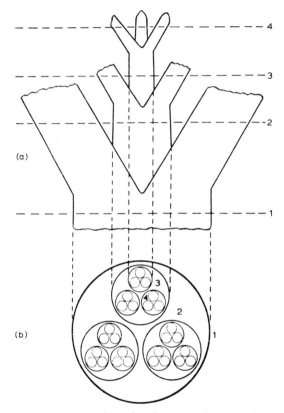

FIG. 28. A cross section of Arthur Koestler's "Holon." "Two ways of diagramming a hierarchy of 4 levels with a 'span' of 3 on each level; (a) the tree; (b) the Chinese box, derived from a cross-section through level 4 of the tree." From Arthur Koestler and J. R. Smythies, *Beyond Reductionism.* Reprinted by permission of A. D. Peters & Co. Ltd.

ments" (p. 204). But the hierarchy is open ended "at the top," because it can be "extended indefinitely": "When the chess player stares at the board in front of him, trying to visualize various situations three moves ahead, he is guided by feedbacks from imagined environments. Most of our thinking, planning and creating operates in such imaginary environments" (p. 205). Observe here that whether it be a Cartesian meditation about the indefiniteness of the universe or a chess analogy about planning strategies, an epistemology of logical types constrains an assumption about a hypothetical dimension, an imaginary environment, which is not 'in' real space but is a logical extrapolation from the 'lower' class.

In order to summarize the contexts of open systems, let us agree with Gyorgy Kepes:

> Each physical form, every living form, every pattern of feeling or thought has its own identity, its boundaries, its extension and its wider context; it contains or is contained by another pattern; it follows or is followed by another pattern. The unique identity, discrete shape, and nature of the space-occupying substance are shaped by the boundary that separates it from and connects it to the space outside. An organic form lives and grows only through its intricate transactions with its environment. An optical event becomes a visually perceived figure only when seen against its ground. The quality, feeling, and meaning of a sound is cast in the matrix of the physical processes that generated it; it is not independent of its surrounding silence or the other sounds that frame it. In the same way, the physical, biological, or moral individuality of man is the function of its active relationship with the physical and social environment.[21]

The semiotic rule of four-dimensional boundaries is therefore, as we noticed in the Introduction, that every act of limitation requires a transcendence; every creation delimits itself as a special case of an implied context of figure-ground relationships.

Self-regulating Mechanisms

Despite the ongoing usefulness of the tree as a model, its metaphorical power as an organism is notoriously untrustworthy in broad applications, because its very vividness as an image can impose unnecessary botanical constraints upon the hypothetical problem to be constructed. Also, the neutrality of logical types yields the same advantages of classes and levels without the authoritarian connotations of hierarchy. By discussing the other kinds of self-regulating mechanisms, we can continue this brief historical sketch while working toward the construction of a 4D model that avoids the organismic associations of tree models.

Although the idea of self-regulation came into its own with a principle of feedback in information theory, the idea of an eternal helmsman, a *cybernos,* is as old as Thales, as old as the idea of a whole cosmos, self-sufficient and ongoing. Another ancient self-regulating system involved the organization of society. Polybius' system of mixed government, based upon the principle of power balanced among different levels and kinds of government, is perhaps the oldest self-regulating social theory. It was based upon a principle of what we have called ritualization, that all governmental systems deteriorate in time: monarchy deteriorates into tyranny, aristocracy deteriorates into oligarchy, democracy deteriorates into anarchy. Also, a principle of homeostasis was involved: The balance of power among the three branches of government sustains the whole while impeding the deteriorization of any one of the three subassemblies. The system therefore had its own built-in governor, a self-balancing principle designed to withstand the deterioration of the body politic. It may be misleading, however, to use streamlined terminology such as homeostasis to describe the mixed form of government. Perhaps Ortega y Gasset comes closer to its inception when he compares the form to a fixture of old apothecary shops:

> You know what *Therica Maxima* is—when all hope in mendicants has been lost, the doctor decided to put all the principal mendicants together in a single potion. . . . As you see, this "maximum antidote" was invented in a state of despair about any single medicine. In the political field the mixed constitution serves the same purpose.[22]

Social institutions of all kinds are formulated by a longing for stability, but Polybius' still remains self-balancing.

Perhaps Anaximander constructed the first automated three-dimensional model.[23] His astronomical model was no less marvelous in his era, though certainly cruder, than Archimedes' self-moving model which even showed eclipses of the sun and moon (pp. 82–91). If the principles of automation and of steam were commonplace among the ancient Greeks, why were they reluctant or unable to harness that power for anything other than amusing diversions or scientific meditations? The standard answer, according to Brumbaugh, is that slave power was sufficient to do the work, but he maintains the actual reason to be that the "inventor's mentality had not yet appeared" (p. 91). The juncture between geometrical thinking and mechanical advantage may have been partially rifted by a philosophical disdain on the part of Plato and his Pythagorean followers. For them, only the human soul was self-moving, and automated substitutes were moved merely by the mechanics of transmitted motion. Then too, there were Hippocratic treatises on joints which contain remarks about the apparatus for reducing dislocation being "so powerful" that if one wanted to use it for doing evil rather than good, he would have an irresistible force at his disposal.[24] That ethical grace of not-knowingness was matched by the lack of a necessary increment: the crank was apparently a medieval invention. As noted by Lynn White, of the two kinds of motion, reciprocal and rotary, the crank is required to connect them.[25] For White, the crank is an invention second in importance only to the wheel, but it was a device unknown to the Greeks and Romans.

In the absence of a functional semiotics for dislocating one form of motion to another (and the crank is precisely semiotic in its incorporation of exchange-with-displacement), principles of automation as well as mechanical advantage could not be extensively applied in classical times.

In Chapter 1 we suggested that modeling in three dimensions came of age in the 'pure' sciences with the work of Watson and Crick, yet the most practical modeler in four dimensions lived much earlier. The eighteenth-century craftsman, James Watt, characteristically used working models as he turned the mechanical advantage of steam into innovative engines. His career vis à vis steam began when he was asked by the College of Glasgow to repair a malfunctioning steam engine (Figure 29).[26] Prior to the request Watt had no working experience with steam engines. As he said later, "I set about repairing the model as mere mechanician" (p. 33). Unrestricted by the conventions of the type, which might have narrowed his own fresh perspective, Watt developed a modification for the model that would subsequently revolutionize the steam industry. In the faulty model, and in all other full-scale engines hitherto, the cylinder was required to do a two fold job, each principle of which impeded the working of the other. At the beginning of each stroke of the piston the cylinder should be boiling hot so that the force of the entering steam would not be lost by condensation. However, at the end of the stroke, in order to produce the necessary vacuum, the cylinder had to be lowered to a temperature of about sixty degrees Fahrenheit. He reconciled the conflict, both of keeping the cylinder heated and of condensing the steam, by modeling a separate condenser. As Watt described the solution of May 1765, ". . . the idea came into my mind, that as steam was an elastic body it would rush into a vacuum, and if communication was made between the cylinder and an exhausted vessel, it would rush into it, and might there be condensed without cooling the cylinder" (p. 36). Figure 30 shows Watt's original soldered tin model of a cylinder and the separate condenser which would subsequently accelerate the Industrial Revolution. Exchange-with-displacement at that point was employed in a semiotics of physical power.

There is not space here to describe further Watt's many engineering inventions, almost all of which began with miniature working models that are still preserved. But it is necessary to

FIG. 29. Faulty model of a steam engine repaired by James Watt. Copyright © by the Hunterian Museum, University of Glasgow.

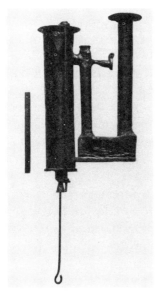

FIG. 30. Watt's original model of a condenser for improving a steam engine. Photo. Science Museum, London.

suggest in passing that his development of rotary engines, cranks, parallel motion devices, and governors might well be a part of an elementary course in kinematics for young people, and not simply the preserve of engineering students. Watt's education of his eldest son, James Watt, Jr., made him the first professional engineering student; yet if miniature working models were similarly made available to children, the models would then become preliminary meditations in their own personal history of discovery. If the physical laws of motion were employed first in plastic assembly models and then in workable steam engines, the mysterious theory of mechanical advantage could be solved by thinking fingers that mesh angles with arcs by way of template assemblages that combine by dislocating rotary and reciprocal motion.

Although Watt is at times erroneously credited with the invention of the centrifugal governor, he was indisputably first in applying it to a steam engine (pp. 153–55). In 1788 he developed a machine that had two heavy metal balls attached to a vertical shaft by a linkage that allowed them to fly outward by centrifugal motion as the engine speed increased. That action raised a throttle valve to the steam pipe, thereby diminishing the steam and reducing the engine until an equilibrium was attained. The governor therefore worked as a self-regulating device, much like a thermostat in one's living room, the analogy used in most introductions to feedback.

Four-dimensional semiotics, the study of Class D instruments, would therefore employ the language of cybernetics or of systems theory as the discourse of its fullest study. Thomas Sebeok has indicated how this discipline might be used:

> . . . the genetic code must be regarded as the most fundamental of all semiotic networks and therefore as the prototype for all other signaling systems used by animals, including man. From this point of view, molecules that are quantum systems, acting as stable physical information carriers, zoosemiotic systems, and, finally, cultural systems, comprehending language, constitute a natural sequence of stages of ever more complex energy levels in a single universal evolution. It is possible, therefore, to describe language from a unified cybernetic standpoint.[27]

In concluding this chapter we can construct epistemological diagrams that will depict the possibilities and problematics of such a unified standpoint.

Conclusion

The movement described thus far as "holism" has not had its lack of detractors. The opponents' method is usually described as "reductionism" by holists, a pejorative term for the empirical method, wherein the subassemblies of a system are reduced to parts and scrutinized in isolation from the rest of their environment.[28] Perhaps the most forceful recent rebuttal to the holists has been Jacques Monod, whose analysis of microscopic cybernetic systems attacks the holists on their safest ground, the discipline of biology.[29] According to Monod, their challenge of the analytical approach is "foolish and wrongheaded," because it misapprehends the critical role that dissection of components must play in understanding the function of the whole organism. In fact, Monod maintains that it is only by way of analysis that the goal of the holists can be achieved: "On such a basis, but not on that of a vague 'general theory of system,' it becomes possible for us to grasp in what very real sense the organism does effectively transcend physical laws—even while obeying them—thus achieving at once the pursuit and fulfillment of its own purpose" (p. 80).

With that harsh caveat in mind, let us begin to construct a diagram (in Figure 31) that will begin to include both methods of analysis and synthesis. Both methods are interested in system, but from different perspectives. As Monod's colleague, Francois Jacob, explains the difference, in *The Logic of Life,* reductionism examines "the system formed by each living being," while "integrationism," as he calls "holism," "considers living beings as the elements of a vast system embracing the whole earth."[30] In the foreground of Figure 31 is the integrationist perspective; in the background is the reductionist. First we see that both perspectives are capable of infinite regressions from the next higher boundary to an assumed context. By way of analytic cutting tools (Class A instruments) one eventually succeeds to the current most elemental building block inside the nucleus of an atom. By way of synthetic combining tools, one then contains the figure in ever more inclusive grounds or fields, retreating at last to the horizon of the most fitting cosmological theory. Since in semiotics we say that any sign is a relation between the signifier and the

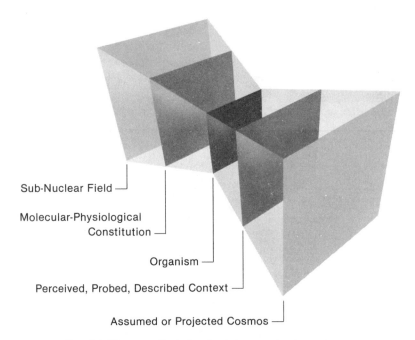

Sub-Nuclear Field ⌐

Molecular-Physiological
Constitution ⌐

Organism ⌐

Perceived, Probed, Described Context ⌐

Assumed or Projected Cosmos ⌐

FIG. 31. Diagram depicting both integrationist and reductionist methods of discovery.

signified, we may say that reductionism examines the systematic
relations *within* an organism or object, thereby giving priority to
the figure; whereas integrationism explores the systematic relations *between* an organism or object and its assumed context, with
prominence given to the ground. In both regressive perspectives,
we shall observe that form becomes content to the next 'higher'
level, while each higher level is a function of the lower's structure.
Since each level may be construed as a horizontal slice, or synchrony, that summons up phantasms of purely spatial horizons,
let us modify the model so that it begins to include a temporal
dimension, thereby allowing a cybernetic interaction between the
different levels.

Instead of using a variant of Chinese boxes, let us construct a pair of interpenetrating cones as in Figure 32. The broad-based cone will represent the kind of discovery which confirms presuppositions according to the logic of what Thomas S. Kuhn has called "normal science."[31] We shall not denigrate those studies, because they verify elements according to the accepted paradigm, and so isolate a remainder of unverifiable issues that require a leap to another principle of confirmation, which we have represented as an inverted cone. Once we decide to make the two

Fig. 32. Diagram of two interpenetrating cones which suggests the meeting of two kinds of discovery.

cones mutually penetrating, so as to avoid the illusion that the second order of confirmation is hierarchically better than the broad-based cone, other advantages accrue. It is sometimes presumed that in a hierarchically organized system the higher level contains the code that deciphers the message of the lower level; or more traditionally that the higher level is form to the lower level's content. For instance, the rules of syntax cannot be extrapolated from the lower level of grammar, just as methods of writing a paragraph cannot be derived from the laws of syntax. Nor can the felicities of a good style be derived from rules for constructing a paragraph. That kind of hierarchical thinking reckons without the presuppositions of the broad-based cone. One must simultaneously draw upon the stored knowledge of each level so that the various codes point toward the final message. For instance, if one wishes to understand the specific environment probed by an amoeba, he must understand the perceptual limits of the amoeba's physiology. In other words, the integrationist and reductive methods are mutually necessary and are in fact complementary aspects of one need. But as with perspectives upon space and time, one aspect is displaced from consideration even as we use its attributes to highlight the other. Such indeterminacy is an extrapolation of semiotic exchange-with-displacement. Hence a more adequate rendition of the methods for solving a problem would be to imagine one's searching stance as being at the midpoint of the interpenetrating cones, where there is a circle that is geometrically congruent. No matter what stage one happens to be in while solving a problem, he will be at some midpoint where the two perspectives are being simultaneously drawn upon; retrieving and sending, excluding and including choices.

If we now transform the cones into spirals, as in Figure 33, we can then depict the kinematic circuitry needed for various four-dimensional systems. The central circle of the cone in Figure 32 now becomes a pair of congruent helices, where the incoming and outgoing messages converge. Each cone is represented as being strapped by two spiral bands going in opposite directions, because in both modes of discovery, one is predicting and recapitulating, drawing back in order to leap higher. The central helix could represent a thermostat in the classic example of a feedback mechanism. On another occasion the helix could represent the desired equipose of any organism that must maintain an equilibrium between inputs from an environment and outputs from itself. It could also represent a dialog of speaking and listening, where sound and sense are reciprocally initiated by each sender and receiver. Also, as a model of discovery, the pair of helices at the center combines the inductive thinking of the pyramidal phrase "is based on," which we discussed in Chapter 1, with the deductive method of search-lighting 'higher' helices in the conjectural mode.

In his *Structuralism,* Piaget imagined a similar spiral in order to depict the revolutionary paradox in Kurt Gödel's 1931 paper regarding consistency in confirmation:

> Gödel showed that the construction of a demonstrably consistent relatively rich theory requires not simply an "analysis" of its "presuppositions," but the construction of the next "higher" theory! Previously, it was possible to view theories as layers of a pyramid, each resting on the one below, the theory at ground level being the most secure because constituted by the simplest means, and the whole firmly posed upon a self-sufficient base. Now, however, "simplicity" becomes a sign of weakness and the "fastening" of any theory in the edifice of human knowledge calls for the construction of the next higher theory. To revert to our earlier image, the pyramid of knowledge no longer rests on foundations but hangs by its vertex, an ideal point reached and, more curious, constantly rising! In short, rather than envisaging human knowledge as a pyramid or building of some sort, we should think of it as a spiral the radius of whose turns increases as the spiral rises.[32]

Let us adopt Piaget's widening gyre, but retain the pyramid as well.

If one already has a glimpse of the end of a problem even as he becomes aware that a problem exists, if in the order of desire the end precedes the means, then one of the pair of helices implies that he is looking back upon the problem from the hypothetical dimension of the semiotic model even while he is, in the other helix, striving inductively with analytic means towards that end. In that stance one is therefore exploring the relations within

Fɪɢ. 33. Diagram of interlaced spiral paths which suggests the complementarity of knowing.

and without the system to be learned, so that its solution simultaneously opens out to another horizon while it satisfactorily closes another boundary.

The helix therefore could represent that very human state of imminence, where one is always on the verge of stasis, but not quite. We have reached a state that John Dewey calls "rhythm." His definition includes the complementarity of opposite methods that we have depicted in the diagram:

> Esthetic recurrence in short is a vital, physiological, function. Relationships rather than elements recur, and they recur in differing contexts and with different consequences so that each recurrence is novel as well as a reminder. In satisfying an aroused expectancy, it also institutes a new longing, incites a fresh curiosity, establishes a changed suspense. The completeness of the integration of these two offices, opposed as they are in abstract conception, by the *same* means instead of by using one device to arouse energy and another to bring it to rest, measures artistry of production and perception. A well-conducted scientific inquiry discovers as it tests, and proves as it explores; it does so in virtue of a method which combines both functions. And conversation, drama, novel, and architectural construction, if there is an ordered experience, reach a stage that at once records and sums up the value of what precedes, and evokes and prophesies what is to come. Every closure is an awakening, and every awakening settles something. This state of affairs defines organization of energy.[33]

The well-constructed four-dimensional model provides that rhythmic impetus.

Conclusion:
On Semiotic
Acceleration

> To conclude, Expansion and Duration do mutually embrace, and comprehend each other; every part of Space, being in every part of Duration; and every part of Duration in every part of Expansion. Such a combination of two distinct Ideas is, I suppose, scarce to be found in all of that great Variety, we do or can conceive, and may afford Matter to further Speculation.[1]

Following Locke's supposition, very few philosophers speculated substantially about the union of space and time until the early twentieth century, but now it seems fair to say that the phenomenon which most often characterizes modernism is some variable of expansion and duration combined, a phenomenon of acceleration. For several reasons, acceleration pertains to our task of introducing the dimensionality of signs. Acceleration is a dimensional way of expressing an observed torsion in space and time, where the two increments "mutually embrace one another." Furthermore, acceleration is expressed as an exponential increase in rates of exchange. Perhaps most important, acceleration of human products, of human numbers, of semiotic equipment itself, may be seen as the primary vehicle for increasing that state of alienation which most often defines humans. So what might be a semiotic perspective upon the dimensionality of acceleration, and of its result, alienation?

According to a number of thinkers of otherwise different persuasion, an acceleration in tempo is the crux of modernism. A revolutionary rate of change is an awareness which springs from the revolutionary rate of exchange of goods and services that we call the Industrial Revolution. (In this regard, a theory of change is an index of semiotic exchange.) For E. J. Hobsbawm, this "take-off into self-sustained growth" was a "revolution," not simply an "accelerated evolution"; and from the 1780s onward the norm of transformation has been "revolutionary change."[2] For Frank E. Manuel, "that acceleration in tempo in all phases of economic life" characterizes the British system during the Industrial Revolution.[3] Our task here is not to plumb the origins of that revolution; ours is the simpler task of observing the distortions that arise when expansion and duration are accelerated together. For distortion is aggravated torsion. In the context of expansion and duration considered together, what is the precise relation between the expansion of products or services of industry and the apparent acceleration in tempo that accompanies the multiplication of goods?

Perhaps the most exhaustive argument relating a "law of acceleration" to the dilemma of modernism via the expansion of goods is found in the works of Henry and Brooks Adams.[4] Henry Adams' version of the law has peculiar pertinence to our semiotic concerns, because he expressed his law as a variable of the inverse-square law, discussed in Chapter 3. For Henry Adams, the several phases of economic history may be gauged by temporal demarcations ruled by successive inverse-squares:

> Supposing the Mechanical Phase to have lasted 300 years, from 1600 to 1900, the next or Electric Phase would have a life equal to $\sqrt{300}$, or about seventeen years and a half, when—that is, in 1917—it would pass into another or Ethereal Phase, which, for half a century, science has been promising, and which would last only $\sqrt{17.5}$ or about four years, and bring Thought to the limit of its possibilities in the year 1921.[5]

Is this analogy between numerical laws of thermodynamics and the history of human productivity an absurd yoking? Henry Adams' large conjecture is that a person with a common-sense education of the eighteenth century cannot hope to cope with the age of the Dynamo, that "the limits of [mental] expansion"

(*Education*, p. 396) will soon be reached. Since the presence of acceleration is described by a curved line, Adams saw that his law of accelerated phases could be diagrammed by a curve that resembles the vaporization of water: "The resemblance is too close to be disregarded, for nature loves the logarithm, and perpetually recurs to her inverse-square" (*Degradation*, p. 291). Adams' curve, reproduced here as Figure 34, suggests why the analogy is misleading, when Adams predicted that the limit of thought would be reached. For if one thinks purely in terms of inverse-squares, the end cannot be reached by way of the diagram. One of the oldest mathematical paradoxes, Zeno's about Achilles and the tortoise, explains that Achilles will never overtake the tortoise if he thinks about temporal and spatial demarcations. If he runs twice as fast as the tortoise and the tortoise has a hundred yards head start, then the distance between the two will always be halved. Similarly Adams' temporal phases will continue to be divided into smaller increments, with the boundaries becoming ever more miniscule and meaningless. But the idea of meaninglessness does not carry over to the human condition. Since classification is done only for the convenience of sorting ideas, having no effect really upon the material world but only upon the hypothetical dimension of semiotics, these smaller divisions are merely symptoms of analogical inconvenience.

So Adams' rigorous distortion of an analogy of acceleration allows us to conjecture that from his perspective modernism is not so much an articulated condition as it is a fetish. Measured starkly by a law of acceleration, the human condition is an obsolescent gauge; and the spinning jenny, the flywheel, the dynamo —all products of a speeding economy of means—become themselves signs of human limitations as they contribute to the process of acceleration. Modernism is an idea only in so far as relative motion is an idea. It is not even a philosophy of relativism, because it is governed by an exponential curve of accelerating motion. There is no reason to it, neither relativistic nor

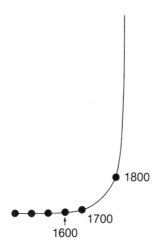

FIG. 34. Logarithmic curve for the acceleration of history. Adapted from Henry Adams, *The Degradation of the Democratic Dogma.*

authoritarian. Modernism is the rule of inverse-squares triumphant. A means to an end has become an end in itself, a fetish similar to the iron coffin that John Wilkinson had built of the material which ruled his life.[6] In fact, Adams himself uses the word "fetish"—"the idea of an occult power to which obedience was due"—in order to describe the classification of phases of history under the aegis of one power or another, such as Comtean phases of polytheistic, monotheistic, metaphysical, mechanical, postivistic, and so forth (*Degradation,* pp. 285–94.)

Zeno's paradoxical chop logic set aside, is acceleration nonetheless a usable sign for gauging the emptiness of modernism? Let us cite Einstein's brief discussion of fetishism as a way of reviewing our own discussion of means and ends.

The instincts bring thought into action, and thought provokes intermediary actions inspired by emotions which are likewise related to the ultimate end. Through repeated performance, this process brings it about that ideas and beliefs acquire and retain a strong effective power even after the ends which gave them that power are long forgotten. In abnormal cases of such intensive borrowed emotions, which cling to objects emptied of their erstwhile effective meaning, we speak of fetishism.[7]

Fetishism is therefore a most surprising regulatory maxim, for it is of a kind with the empty placebo of that species of dance fly which also ritualized purely empty form. A fetish is the worship of a ritualized null set, a category that in time, through means-ends distortion, has become emptied of all meaningful content. Is a modern fetish the idea of "repeated performance" itself, of endless reproduction of semiotic placebos? We recall that the central argument of Cassirer's *Essay on Man* is that humans no longer live in the physical world but rather in a "symbolic universe":

> Physical reality seems to reduce in proportion as man's symbolic activity advances. Instead of dealing with the things themselves man is in a sense constantly conversing with himself. He has so enveloped himself in linguistic forms, in artistic images, in mythical symbols of religious rites that he cannot see or know anything except by the interposition of this artificial medium.[8]

Cassirer's inverse ratio is especially fascinating with respect to the metaphor of an increasingly symbolic envelope. As the ratio becomes more unequal, the physical world is barricaded beyond the pale of symbols, leaving man alone in an empty set. Further along, this idea of fetishism must be reconciled with alienation.

In the history of inverse-square malappropriation, it is necessary to cite two forerunners of Henry Adams who used variations of inverse ratios in order to make conjectures about the future. In Chapter 4 we briefly mentioned a principle of self-regulation inhering in Polybius' system of mixed government. In *The Social Contract*, however, Rousseau formulated a law which must destroy that balance in time.[9] It is a positive law of bodies politic, for Rousseau, that as population increases, the proportion of governing leaders decreases. Rousseau agrees with Montesquieu that republics work only in countries of small population:

> If the size of the population is increased to a hundred thousand, the situation of the subject does not change, for each subject is equally with the rest subordinate to the empire of the laws, while his own single voice, reduced to the hundred-thousandth part, has ten times less influence in the formulation of those laws. Hence, since the subject is always one individual, the proportion in which the sovereign stands to him always increases in relation to the size of the population. From this it follows that the more the state increases, the more liberty diminishes.[10]

Jouvenal shows that as liberty diminishes among the people, authority becomes concentrated in the rulers, until the executive prevails over the legislative branch; "and when the law is finally subordinate to men, there remains nothing but slaves and masters, and the state is destroyed."[11]

If, among other considerations, mathematics may be defined as the method of saying more and more with fewer numbers of signs, of being simultaneously comprehensive and compact, then Rousseau's 'law', with Adams' 'law', is a similar expression of an extreme of ritualization. Any ratio of inverse proportions yields the potential for an indefinite regress toward either 'end', toward the infinitesimal and toward the infinite. Rousseau's law ends with Caesarism, with an inverse proportion betwixt the one and the many. A law of inverse proportion, wherein more and more is said about stuff with fewer and fewer signifiers, is an extreme achievement of semiotics. Elements of the material world set aside, the set of signifiers that inversely combine the one and the many is the ultimate semiotic formula. But we must always remember that the inverse threat demeans such achievement: that more and more semiotic equipment can be brought to bear in order to discover or to control less and less of the physical world. This aspect of the modernist dilemma we must also discuss further on.

A related eighteenth-century effort to impose mathematical law upon large populations was of course Thomas Robert Malthus' principle of population.[12] Rousseau had been a house guest of his father, and the younger Malthus had been educated in an advanced manner. It was in opposition to a conversation in which his father had advanced William Godwin's euphoric celebration of human progress that the son used mathematics to refute such blithe futurism. As everyone knows, Malthus simply juxtaposed two ratios—the arithmetical increase of agricultural products as against the geometrical increase of human population—in order to counter the optimism of future betterment:

> Taking the population of the world at any number, a thousand millions, for instance, the human species would increase in the ratio of—1, 2, 4, 8, 16, 32, 64, 128, 256, 512, &c. and subsistence as— 1, 2, 3, 4, 5, 6, 7, 8, 9, 10, &c. In two centuries and a quarter, the population would be to the means of subsistence as 512 to 10, in three centuries as 4096 to 13, and in two thousand years the difference would be almost incalculable, though the produce in that time would have increased to an immense extent (Chapter 2).

Appleman in his Preface says of this check that Malthus "saw no real hope for permanent improvement, because he thought of the ratios as representing a law of nature as immutable as Newton's" (p. xvii).

Both for Rousseau and for Malthus, the formal cause of their laws was an acceleration in populace, and thus the pressure of crowding. Crowding into cities created for Rousseau the unnatural constraints that made humans do evil; for Malthus, crowding simply induced famine as a restraint. As a result of increase in population of people and their products, crowding is therefore the chief agent of that Hegelian phenomenon where at a certain point an increase in quantity affects quality.

But is theirs an "immutable" law of nature? When there occurs in nature an increase of population within a constrained environment, then folding usually occurs so that the enlargement might continue. For D'Arcy Thompson such foldings characterize one of the most visible constancies in nature: a constant ratio between body surface and volume is maintained through changes in form.[13] Examples are folds in the lining of intestines and the development of villi upon lining. "A leafy wood, a grassy sward, a piece of sponge, a reef of coral, are all instances of a like phenomenon." Furthermore, the ratio between growth and form among large organisms is regulated by the pressure of gravity (p. 36), so an inverse-square law manifests itself. But what is the difference between the pressure of gravity and the pressure of crowding among organisms of the same species? On the surface of the earth gravity is everywhere uniform, but in cases where organisms crowd one another by adjacency, as with coral colonies, instead of action at a distance, then the pressure must be measured differently. So we shall not hastily assert that the inverse-square law may be uniformly applied, even though nature might love the logarithm. But it is helpful to characterize Rousseau's and Malthus' laws as kinds of grotesque three-dimensional topology in which 'over and under' knotting is expressed mathematically as a law of inverse proportion, and in which some manifestation of pressure is the formal cause.

The elegance of D'Arcy Thompson's thinking, especially in his chapter "On Magnitude," springs from his understanding of scale: "Everywhere Nature works true to scale, and everything has its proper size accordingly" (p. 17). Scale is an expression of the ratio of everything with its environment; in that regard the acceleration of populace for Rousseau and Malthus demanded conjectures about the possibilities of scale for disproportionate growth. Dimensionality itself had grown monstrous with the necessity for expressing population in terms of mass numbers. A dimensionality of gigantism was needed, but who could understand it? Henry Adams felt that even the elegance of mathematics could not assuage his modernist confusion over principles of the "electro-magnetic school":

> The average man, in 1850, could understand what Davy or Darwin had to say; he could not understand what Clerk Maxwell meant. The later terms were not translatable into the earlier; even the mathematics became hyper-mathematical. Possibly a physicist might go so far as to hold that the most arduous intellectual effort ever made by man with a distinct consciousness of needing new mental powers was made after 1870 in the general effort to acquire habits of electro-magnetic thought,—the familiar use of formulas carrying indefinite self-contradiction into the conception of force.[14]

Laying aside questions about the relativism of common sense for each era, we may sympathize with Adams' fear that the acceleration expressed vividly by the logarithmic curve meant a monstrous collapse of the dimensionality of space and time as he knew it. His sense of scale was violated by the monstrous power of thermodynamics.

In the context of accelerating tempos and of the average man's increasingly inadequate understanding, Heidegger's lament about timeliness makes special sense; he ends *An Introduction to Metaphysics* in a manner similar to our speculation about disproportionate growth:

> To know how to question means to know how to wait, even a whole lifetime. But an age which regards as real only what goes fast and can be clutched with both hands looks on questioning as "remote from reality" and as something that does not pay, whose benefits cannot be numbered. But the essential is not number; the essential is the right time, i.e. the right moment and the right perseverance.
> "For," as Holderlin said, "the mindful God abhors untimely growth." ("Aus dem Motivkreis der Titanen," *Samtliche Werke* 4, p. 218.)[15]

Products of untimely growth are enormities. What Hamlet learned about the timeliness of action, "The readiness is all," is similar to Holderlin's expression; but amidst the rush of modernism, for Adams and for Heidegger, acceleration makes one obsolescent before one is ready to act.

Obsolescence is another way of describing the paradoxical quality of "fleetingness" that characterizes the products of the Industrial Revolution. Products of labor are almost immediately consumed; what then can be the sign of their elapsed value other than the "lasting" quality of money? Hannah Arendt shows that Locke, Marx, and Veblen have all focused upon the absurdity of immediately consuming products of labor.[16] Acceleration, we recall, is not simply an increase in speed, but may also be a decrease, as in deceleration. So obsolescence in this regard is the complement to the ephemerality of consumed products, being the apparent measure of unconsumed products, as well as of the labor force, which apparently has decelerated in usefulness as the tempo of other new goods has increased.

Edward O. Wilson uses an analogy from the natural world to describe cultural acceleration. Autocatalysis is the "process in which the products of a reaction serve as catalysts, that is, they speed up the rate of the same reaction that produced them and cause it to accelerate."[17] We shall hesitate from using this otherwise scintillating analogy, because catalysts remain chemically unchanged even as they contribute to the reaction. A catalyst is like the sprite Ariel in Shakespeare's play *The Tempest:* it contributes to the acceleration of tempo in that play which is about timing, but otherwise it remains inherently unchanged by the events. In that acceleration of culture which we call modernism, the instruments of new technology themselves are characterized by fleetingness; unlike catalysts, they quickly become obsolete themselves. Perhaps the phrase from information theory, "positive feedback," used by Gunther Stent, more neutrally describes that cycle of accelerating reactions caused by the reentry of the product into the original process. Both analogies nicely describe the semiotic dilemma of modernism. Following some thousands of years of slowly innovative products, the Industrial Revolution accelerated the process of production so that now some feel crowded by their own prostheses. Instead of probing for us, like Niels Bohr's walking stick, symbolic constructions, for some thinkers about technology, have become busy distractions that impede one from the spare life. Omnipresent in their envelopment, yet fleeting in their turnover, semiotic products in an economy of means seem to be curious inversions of expansion and duration considered together.

Apparently the social need for semiotics as a discipline of study arises from the awareness that signs, of all dimensions, can divert attention from basic issues. Paul Garvin cites the Czech thinker, Jan Mukařovský, who expressed the possibility and the problem of semiotics some forty years ago:

> We live in a period with tremendous emphasis on signs: social, economic and political organizations have developed in the last decades to such a degree of complexity that the only way to control them is by means of signs standing in lieu of realities, in many cases even by means of a multilayered hierarchy of signs (signs of signs). Thus, for instance, economists are beginning to realize the increasing importance of the purely symbolic character of money as currencies are gradually detached from their strict dependence on the metal base which used to link money to a material reality. The increasing importance of the sign is necessary and inevitable, but it also has its drawbacks; in many cases we aren't able to manage signs adequately, largely because we don't know the sign in all of the complexity of its structure and function: semiology, the science of signs, which Saussure called for with so much foresight, is still in its bare beginnings.[18]

If, as some have said, mankind is nothing other than evolution become conscious of itself, semiotics is the discipline that as a product of increasing populations, both cultural and genetic, is self-conscious about its task to understand from whence symbol making has come and whither it might be taking us. If semiotics is a corollary of accelerating populations, then it takes its rise with the discipline of statistics, which itself appeared at the same time as did the Malthusian need to cope with the significance of anonymously vast populations. According to Jouvenal, the "Average Man," a phrase used by Adams above, was coined by De Quetelet in an era (1832) when the pressure of numbers was becoming increasingly apparent.[19] To the degree that individualism tended to be effaced by the press of population, the Average Man anonymously substituted for the individual in a hypothetical dimension of statistics, perhaps with the same inverse ratio posed by Rousseau in terms of social freedom. As semiotic products accelerated, the craftsman was transformed into an anonymous laborer.

For Gunther Stent, however, an inverse ratio of "diminishing returns" now characterizes the results of an accelerating technology bent to the task of discovering the new. In most disciplines, the frontiers of the natural world have been all but conquered. In his chapter "The End of the Arts and Sciences," Stent maintains that the secrets of the central nervous system will be solved in the next twenty years, making that system as understandable then as the knowledge of heredity is at present. Even the open-endedness of physics is limited by the limitations of human intellect. Like Henry Adams, Stent believes that "common sense" becomes alienated by the unnatural abstractions of quantum or of universal physics.[20] Hence in all disciplines an end of "progress" is at hand.

Semiotic Alienation

Stent's exhaustion of interest in further discovery is part of that temporal form of alienation in which the eighteenth-century man of common sense feels left behind, feels obsolete, by the acceleration of new products which themselves seem to be less and less useful. The situation is not without irony. For in the discussion of the phenomenon of inverse proportions we remember that Rousseau, Malthus, and Adams, each in his own way, resorted to a law that depends upon illogical paradox for its allure. The paradox of inverse proportion varies from common sense as the phenomenon of $\sqrt{2}$ first offended the sensible world of whole numbers for the Pythagoreans.[21] Alienation is very old. All three of our principals were exponents of new educational methods, and all three used the arcaneries of mathematics in order to express their disillusionment with the acceleration of culture. In Adams' case, especially, it seems that the dynamic modernism of his own proof discounted his plea of exhaustion. What is more 'modern' than an inverse-square law of historical phases? The sting of alienation apparently prompted an avant-garde theory that exploited his eighteenth-century understanding, following Locke and Hume, of the natural limits to human understanding.

Alienation is a term of such inflated currency that perhaps its use should be entirely avoided. For as Raymond Williams says, "Alienation is now one of the most difficult words in the language."[22] Nevertheless, there exists a need for the word, just as the state itself, we shall conjecture, is needed. For alienation is an expression of the human condition. Perhaps alienation is not intrinsically an evil, if it prompts a Henry Adams, though its accelerated state certainly measures a crowded and 'pressed' culture. But first let us be more precise in defining alienation. Let us place it first in a large historical context, of which Karl Marx is the most prodigious example. A definition that most usefully accords with the means and ends of human instrumentation is Isaiah Berlin's use of the term in his description of Marx's work:

> For him alienation (for that is what Hegel, following Rousseau and Luther and an earlier Christian tradition, called the perpetual self-divorce of men from unity with nature, with each other, with God, which the struggle of thesis against antithesis entailed) is intrinsic to the social process, indeed it is the heart of history itself. Aliena-

tion occurs when the results of men's acts contradict their true purposes, when their official values, or the parts they play, misrepresent their real motives and needs and goals. This is the case, for example, when something that men have made to respond to human needs—say, a system of laws, or the rules of musical composition—acquires an independent status of its own, and is seen by men, not as something created by them to satisfy a common social want (which may have disappeared long ago), but as an objective law of institution, possessing eternal, impersonal authority in its own right, like the unalterable laws of Nature as conceived by scientists and ordinary men, like God for a believer.[23]

The passage is cited at length neither for rebuttal nor for expansion, but rather to set forth the currency of alienation in the history of human issues. Indeed its very scope—re. history of names cited, re. question of nature, re. human motives at large —suggests the effrontery of approaching the issue head on. It can, however, be approached semiotically, that is, obliquely. For the alienation of human products, as well as human beings, as we shall see, is the radical result of exchange with displacement. Strangely enough, that "independent status" which a composition may achieve might just as well define a fetish such as the capitalist system in Marx's view, or a model of discovery where a tool may be viewed as an apparent end in itself, or as an art work in the 'anti-context' of art for art's sake. What is the necessity of alienation with respect to these products of ritualization? What is the relation between alienation and fetishism?

Isaiah Berlin describes alienation almost exactly as Adams had earlier described fetishism:

The symptom of alienation is the attribution of ultimate authority, either to some impersonal power—say the laws of supply and demand—from which the rationality of capitalism is represented as being logically reducible, or to imaginary persons or forces—divinities, churches, the mystical person of the king or priest, or interims of other oppressive myths, whereby men, torn from a 'natural' mode of life (which alone makes it possible for entire societies to perceive the truth and live harmoniously), seek to explain their unnatural condition to themselves (p. 140).

If the symptom of alienation is that attribution of authority to which men explain their unnatural condition to themselves, then alienation is self-conscious fetishism. For fetishism is worship without being aware that the fetish is a placebo. (Recall that Berlin's first passage shares with Einstein's passage the metaphor of 'empty' form with respect to the "disappearance" in time of an original social need.) Alienation therefore is a semiotic awareness of improper signification, of misassignment. And semiotics is a discipline that is self-conscious about the acceleration of disfunctional signs.

Let us set aside for a moment the long history of human alienation from nature because of improper signification, and instead let us think of alienation as the act of surmounting need by way of an exchange of products or ideas. If the primary meaning of alienation is a state of permanent estrangement, a secondary meaning is the transfer of ownership to another. Furthermore, the most general definition of "alienation" in *The Oxford English Dictionary* is the "Diversion of anything to a different purpose." Now that definition economically defines the essentials of semiotics, if indeed exchange-with-displacement is the issue. Perhaps we are now in a position to assert that the primary meaning of estrangement depends upon the secondary meaning of diversionary exchange. For to make one feel alien is to convert or transform one into a stranger; the act of permanent diversion can result in permanent alienation, as this eighteenth-century rime about The Enclosure Acts makes clear:

The law condemns the man or woman
Who steals the goose from off the common
But leaves the greater fellow loose
Who steals the common from off the goose!

Pulling the ground out from underneath the figure of the goose is an act of metaphorical diversion that transforms the feeling of alienation into burlesque. Nonetheless it is alienation, not fetishism, for the rimester here exposes the law as being without power. The rimester knows that power flows from the land (from ground) and not from symbolic ascription of authority. When the Mad Hatter told Alice the difference between "I said what I meant" and "I meant what I said," he exposed the nonsense of ordinary semiotic reversals. "I said what I meant" is fetishism; the reverse is alienation.

The eighteenth-century rimester reversed ordinary figure-ground relationships. Only a fool would kill the goose that laid the golden eggs. Common law and common sense could not imagine the greater knave who would steal the ground itself, thereby alienating all further agricultural products. Stealing is that extreme act of risky diversion which deliquesces profits as well as the source of profits. Then too, the removal of the common from under the goose reified the goose. The German word for reification, *Vergegenständlichung*, ponderously exposes the nice Gestalt relationship in the rime. As Hannah Arendt says, the word *Gegenstand* means "object"; more literally, it means "something thrown" or "put against."[24] So when one might say that the goose has been reified, he does not mean that she has been simply abstracted, but also that her environment has been taken away and she exists subsequently as an "object" in an objective world without other relationship to that ground which previously under-stood her.[25]

Gegenstand, the prepositional quality of an object being defined in contrast to its ground, its *erthe,* as we discussed it in Chapter 1, helps to explain the sudden alienation of the hideous frog into the handsome prince. According to the Brothers Grimm, the princess angrily threw the frog against her bedroom wall when he insisted upon climbing into bed with her. But then it arose transformed into the prince. Being thrown 'over against' the wall metaphorically plays upon the transformation of objects as different environs induce changed identities. Changes in identity are defined "by contrast." Cinderella's slipper, that sign of another order of reality, is "glass" only because of an unintentional mistranslation of the more prosaic "gold" slipper. The intentional use of this kind of alienation is enacted upon the original analyst of the signifier "Wall." When Bottom suddenly appeared with the head of an ass upon his shoulders, Peter Quince exclaimed, "Bless thee, Bottom! bless thee! thou art translated!"

The definition of alienation in sum should include both the process and the products of exchange and of reversal. Since exchange of semiotic figures may involve exchange away from those natal environs which had previously defined those figures, an unintended by-product may be a quality of disembodiment as the sign becomes groundless, like the goose, or is exchanged into an alien ground, like the frog. Furthermore, the apparent feeling of estrangement results from someone who feels disadvantaged by the outcome of a contract that had promised mutual advantage in the exchange. Any contract involves risk, and the risk of capitalist venture, as it prostitutes a Kantian audacity to know, has been explored by Wylie Sypher.[26] But how does alienation enter into the risky task of discovery? Any conjecture about the future, any contract, audaciously places one in an isolate contingency, in harm's way. Alienation might be construed as lapsed risk, where the headiness of conjecture meets the flatness of rebuttal, or in extreme cases, a knavery of dishonest rejoinder. However, the importance of discovery does not reside with the euphoric feeling of the discoverer, but rather in the social exchange of ideas, in the pattern of conjecture and of refutation which is the high seriousness of scholarship.

If one were to discriminate between the relatively isolated task of scientific discovery as averse to the relatively social task of scientific confirmation, then the vexatious stance of scientific objectivity might be more meaningfully construed as the dispassion which effaces alienation. Although the celebrated race to first achieve the structure of the DNA molecule revealed a rowdiness in some of the racers, it must not be forgotten that the point of the race was to find the most fitting model. The indifference of that model, as revealed by Watson in his tale, and as confirmed by those who saw it first, as it stands in itself while re-presenting the other, is a model of scholarly objectivity. That is, the indifference of the model carries with it none of the passionate intensity of its pursuers. It carries no mask and stiletto. It is incurious, like nature.

The state of detached contemplation in which one explores the "fittingness" of a model of discovery is a variant of the esthetic contemplation of beauty. Alienation prompts the desire for beauty insofar as estrangement prompts the desire to be returned to a more fitting environment. But why discuss beauty at all? In the larger context of acceleration and, in particular, the relative fleetingness of semiotic instruments, the beauty of a work of art emanates the permanence of John Keats's Grecian Urn,

> Thou still unravish'd bride of quietness,
> Thou foster-child of silence and slow time, . . .

Let us forego, however, the often discussed question of art's relative lastingness for the less common but more universal observation that beauty shares with the results of model building, as with a *bon mot,* a semiotics of appropriateness. Here we adopt one of the oldest esthetic theories in Western thought, that beauty is a special case of fittingness with the environs of its enactment.

In his *Memoirs,* for instance, Xenophon's discussion of beauty involves our large problem of means-ends analysis. Socrates is there made to say that things are beautiful only so long as they fit their purposes:

"Is a dung basket beautiful then?" "Of course, and a golden shield is ugly, if the one is well made for its special work and the other badly." "Do you mean that the same things are both beautiful and ugly?" "Of course—and both good and bad. For what is good for hunger is often bad for fever, and what is good for fever bad for hunger. . . . For all things are good and beautiful in relation to those purposes for which they are well adapted, bad and ugly in relation to those for which they are ill adapted. . . ."[27]

We observe with Tatarkiewicz that this perspectivism about beauty, in terms of suitability, does not depend relativistically upon an individual's taste. Instead it ennobles proper function. So when we say semiotically that beauty is a special case of fittingness with its surroundings, as a Greek temple sets forth its landscape as ennoblement of that ground, we do not mean that beauty is located spatially 'in' an object as a property of it. That is a version of misplaced concreteness. The semiotic quality of beauty appears to be a quality associated with the rightness of an act in relation to its context. That is to say, beauty is an offshoot of human grace, as when a stranger smiles into a face disfigured by cancer. In this regard goodness and rightness and beauty are indistinguishable.

If beauty is a response to human alienation, then nature is not beautiful, even though it may be appropriated by human act into landscape gardens of rare device. A glorious sunrise upon a misty heath has in its aspect a gratuitous power. Although it may be read as a sign of something else, certainly a sunrise is unintentionally extravagant in itself. As Edmund Burke said once, Nature is "Sublime." Humans feel a complex of passive awe as they are treated to a panorama of power displayed at a distance. The wonderful phenomenon of nature is that randomness causes symmetry. For example, in the random distribution of flotsam on a seashore, groups of similar size and shape are assembled together in patterns. Then too, the formal cause of crowding induces the symmetry of gazelles and zebras, as they are distributed on the veldt. But good artists make symbols which allow us fleetingly to return from alien asymmetry to grace. Nature is characterized everywhere by right scale; it is we who do not fit. In a model that would discover nature, of course, beauty is a secondary consideration of precise matching, as the appropriateness of the model becomes ever closer to the structural codes of the physical world. In a work of art, also, beauty, as in orderliness or grace, may be a secondary consideration to the forceful malappropriation—let us call that malappropriation by the term "alienation"—of Bottom's translation into an ass. Beauty as fittingness therefore is a quality shared both by a model of discovery and by a work of art, though the quality is not limited to either of those hypothetical dimensions.

If beauty is a formulated response to human alienation, then a most beautiful act is the risk that one can take when he or she serves others. Service tends to downplay that instinctive desire which prompts advantageous if-then contracts. In this regard the radical of semiotic exchange is to lay down one's personal life in the place of another's. As Einstein says, "the high destiny of the individual is to serve rather than to rule, or to impose himself in any way."[28] And in "The Dry Salvages" T. S. Eliot further discriminates between the futurism of ordinary desire as averse to the selflessness of service:

> Men's curiosity searches past and future
> And clings to that dimension. But to apprehend
> The point of intersection of the timeless
> With time, is an occupation for the saint—
> No occupation either, but something given
> And taken, in a lifetime's death in love,
> Ardor and selflessness and self-surrender.
> For most of us, there is only the unattended
> Moment, the moment in and out of time, . . .

Scientific discoveries about the physical world, about nature, are processes of revealing the order of what *is* in nature; despite the ardor of conjecture, the stance of scientific verification is one of matter-of-factness, where curiosity becomes one with the indifference of a natural model. That detachment is of a different order than is the curiosity of the humanist, whose stance reveals what *ought* to be 'in' the future, not in nature but in culture. At best, both stances serve a metaphysics of fittingness, in nature and in culture.

The teleology of service is the main issue of means versus ends. We construe semiotics to be a servant to ends that are not baldly instrumental, although it would be impossible to describe those other ends without instruments such as language. Indeed, utopia—the impossible state—requires language with which to ennoble the fiction of the future. It is impossible to get beyond the use of signs, even though intuition, that which precedes and follows articulation, and though faith, that which transcends articulation with silence, are finally beyond the scope of semiotics. And the beauty of those saints who serve with indifference, though not indifferently well, is that they demean themselves and serve others, neither with the expectation that their task will reduce one's alien state, nor that their risk will pay off. The numbers of those who practice true service have not accelerated, even though bureaucracy as a class of public service has increased geometrically. But saints can still be observed at work, despite the inability to count their numbers or gauge their effects semiotically.

If beauty is the response that one feels when human alienation is translated into a special case of fittingness, then nothing is beautiful in itself. Or if one admits to a passion for the crafted beauty of things, one admits to a passion for bric-a-brac, those exponents of no ground but art for art's sake. Unlike baubles and finery, signs, tools, and models always point beyond themselves to the silent environment out of which they were made and "against which" they set forth themselves.[29]

Just as Henry David Thoreau is America's philosopher of manual labor, so his favorite tool was the jack-knife. Emerson reports that Thoreau in his youth once said, "The other world is all my art; my pencils will draw no other; my jack-knife will cut nothing else; I do not use it as a means."[30] In *Walden* similar applications abound, but it is in *Moby Dick* that the metaphorical uses of the jack-knife are most celebrated. The novel is a massive anatomy of the business of whaling as well as the mystery of Leviathan, and the jack-knife is the handy tool that does the anatomizing. In fact the whaling ship's carpenter is likened to "one of those unreasoning but still highly useful, *multum in parvo*, Sheffield contrivances, assuming the exterior—though a little swelled—of a common pocket knife; but containing, not only blades of various sizes, but also screw-drivers, cork-screws, tweezers, awls, pens, rulers, nail files, countersinkers."[31] For Melville, the carpenter is almost pure mechanism, "a stript abstract, an unfractioned integral," whose "brain, if he had ever had one, must have early oozed along into the muscles of his fingers." For our immediate purposes as modelers, the carpenter is himself that tool without parallel, a perfect fit with the world: "For nothing was this man more remarkable, than for a certain impersonal stolidity as it were; impersonal, I say; for it so shaded off into the surrounding infinite of things, that it seemed one with the general stolidity discernable in the whole visible world; which while pauselessly active in accounted modes, still eternally holds its peace, and ignores you, though you dig foundations for cathedrals."

Melville's carpenter, exceptional as a description, describes a commonplace characteristic of humans. One can become so well adapted to one's setting that one becomes absolutely native to it. Such a man does not need to read signs, for he is 'indifferent' as nature; he is unalien. And like nature, he needs to make no predictions; he has no need for semiotics. The all too human ability to adapt, to achieve utter fittingness—with an assembly line, with the settings of situation comedy or soap opera, with the "organization man"—is such a commonplace that it is satirized in the madness of Don Quixote and of Gulliver, both of whom cannot tell the difference between themselves and the environments of which they would become members. Quixote construes a chamber pot to be a helm from romance, and Gulliver ignores his giganticism in Lilliput; so in desiring to be at one with their environs, they fail to read signs of their differences. The desire to achieve utter fittingness is not beauty but grotesquery. Alienation perhaps is not intrinsically an evil, but is a measure of one's interpretation of apartness.

Just as a sign has no value in itself, so beauty has only 'use' value. A thing in itself has only 'in-itselfishness'. However, by means of art or some other excellent human act with signs, tools, or models, beauty accommodates for the state of estrangement, not by denying one's alien state, but by sharing a feeling of aloneness with others. Beauty seems to be a result of semiotic exchange with displacement; it is a moral act of propriety, which springs from an awareness of another's unsuitable condition. From that perspective we see that the significance of beautiful acts looses us from the analogy of acceleration. A right deed forfends the acceleration of waste in time with a different point of departure. As Eliot said toward the close of "The Dry Salvages,"

> And right action is
> Freedom from past and future also.

NOTES

Introduction

1. Thomas Hobbes, *Leviathan*, ed. A. R. Waller (Cambridge: Cambridge University Press, 1908; 1935), p. 11. Parts of this Introduction appeared separately as "The Dimensions of Signs, Tools and Models," *Semiotica*, 28 1/2 (1979): 63–82.

2. See his *Human Nature: On the Fundamental Elements of Policy;* Chapter 4; collected in *Body, Man and Citizen: Thomas Hobbes*, ed. Richard S. Peters (New York: Collier Books, 1967), p. 195. Conjecture is modern in the sense that it emerged with probability theory in the eighteenth century. See Ian Hacking, *The Emergence of Probability* (Cambridge: Cambridge University Press, 1975).

3. Elie Halevy, *The Growth of Philosophic Radicalism* (Boston: Beacon Press, 1955), p. 92.

4. For a brief history of the topic "symbolic space" see Ernst Cassirer, *An Essay on Man* (New Haven: Yale University Press, 1944), pp. 43–55. More recently in various essays now collected in *Objective Knowledge* (New York: Oxford University Press, 1974), Karl R. Popper has theorized about a category that he calls World III, which includes all of the intellectual records of human kind. For its application to physiology see John C. Eccles, *Facing Reality: Philosophical Adventures by a Brain Scientist* (New York: Springer-Verlag, 1970), pp. 164–73. Most pertinent to this introduction is Gerald Holton's "proposition space," which locates in a hypothetical dimension those thematic presuppositions of science that prompt both objective observation and analytic reason. See *Thematic Origins of Scientific Thought: Kepler to Einstein* (Cambridge, Mass.: Harvard Univeristy Press, 1973); and "On the Role of Themata in Scientific Thought," *Science* 188 (25 April 1975): 328–38. See also Thomas A. Sebeok, "Problems in the Classification of Signs," *Studies for Einar Haugen*, ed. Evelyn Scherabon Furchow et al. (The Hague: Mouton, 1972), p. 516.

5. Paul Watzlawick et al., *Change: Principles of Problem Formation and Problem Resolution* (New York: W. W. Norton & Co., 1974), pp. 9–10.

6. Julian S. Huxley, "The Courtship-habits of the Great Crested Grebe (*Podicepts cristatus*); with an addition to the Theory of Sexual Selection," *Proceedings of the . . . Zoological Society of London* 35 (1914): 491–562. For current work in zoosemiotics, see *Animal Communication: Techniques of Study and Results of Research*, ed. Thomas A. Sebeok (Bloomington: Indiana University Press, 1968). An important reexamination of palingenesis is found in Stephen Jay Gould's *Ontogeny and Phylogeny* (Cambridge, Mass: Harvard University Press, 1977).

7. Edward O. Wilson, "Animal Communication," *Scientific American* (September 1972), now collected in *Communication: A Scientific American Book* (San Francisco: W. H. Freeman Co., 1972), p. 35.

8. Konrad Lorenz, *On Aggression*, trans. Marjorie Kerr Wilson (New York: Bantam Matrix Edition, 1966), pp. 57–84. See also Thomas A. Sebeok, "Prefigurements of Art," *Semiotica*, 281/1(1979).

9. Claude Lévi-Strauss, *Tristes Tropiques: An Anthropological Study of Primitive Societies in Brazil*, trans. John and Doreen Weightman (London: Atheneum, 1973), Chapter 25, "A Writing Lesson."

10. G. Lukács, *History and Class Consciousness: Studies in Marxist Dialectics* (Cambridge, Mass.: M.I.T. Press, 1971), pp. 83–222.

11. Roman Jakobson, "Quest for the Essence of Language," *Diogenes* 51 (Fall 1965):36. The entire issue is useful.

12. C. S. Peirce, "The Essence of Mathematics," in *Collected Papers of Charles Sanders Peirce*, ed. Charles Hartshoren and Paul Weiss (Cambridge, Mass.: Harvard University Press, 1933), vol. 4.

13. Alfred North Whitehead, *Science and the Modern World* (New York: Macmillan Free Press, 1925; 1953), p. 21.

14. Translated by C. K. Ogden and I. A. Richards, *The Meaning of Meaning: A Study of the Influence of Language upon Thought and of the Influence of the Science of Symbolism* (New York: Harcourt, Brace and World, Inc., 1923), p. 5. See Ferdinande de Saussure, *Course in General Linguistics*, trans. Wade Baskin (New York: McGraw-Hill Co., 1966).

15. Rudolf Arnheim, *Visual Thinking* (Berkeley: University of California Press, 1969), especially the chapter "Words in Their Place." In ordinary speech also, redundancy is insured by the use of different but parallel codes of discourse such as gesture and inflection. See Gregory Bateson, "Redundancy and Coding," in *Animal Communication*, ed. Thomas A. Sebeok (Bloomington: Indiana University Press, 1968), pp. 614–26. This reinforcement of the message by different codes is called the "ribbon concept" or "multichannel communication" in Sebeok, "Problems in the Classification of Signs," p. 517.

16. Jean Piaget, *The Child's Conception of Space*, trans. F. J. Langdon and J. L. Lunzer (New York: W. W. Norton & Co., 1968), p. 17.

17. Arnheim, p. 180.

18. Johan Huizinga, *Homo Ludens: A Study of the Play Element in Culture* (Boston: Beacon Press, 1955).
19. E. A. Armstrong, "The Crane Dance in East and West," *Antiquity* 17 (1943):71. For an overview see Joseph Needham, *Science and Civilization in China* (Cambridge: Cambridge University Press, 1954), 1:163.
20. See Robert Graves, *The Greek Myths* (New York: Penguin Books Inc., 1955) 1:316–17, for the linkage of hobbling in partridge-dance rituals with Hephaestus (Vulcan) and Tantalus. For Oedipus as Swollen Foot, "walking obliquely," see Lévi-Strauss, "The Structural Study of Myth," trans. Claire Jacobson and Brooke Grundfest Schoepf, in *Structural Anthropology* (New York: Anchor Books, 1963), pp. 214–15.
21. For George Derwent Thomson, *Studies in Ancient Greek Society: The Prehistoric Aegean* (New York: Citadel Press, 1965), 1:121, this clan emblem is but one of many "totemic survivals."
22. For a discussion and a bibliography, see William G. Madsen, "Earth the Shadow of Heaven: Typological Symbolism in *Paradise Lost,*" in *Milton: Modern Essays in Criticism,* ed. Arthur E. Barker (New York: Oxford University Press, 1965), pp. 246–63.
23. José Ortega y Gasset, *The Dehumanization of Art and Other Essays on Art, Culture and Literature* (Princeton: Princeton University Press, 1968), p. 33.
24. Sigmund Freud, *Civilization and Its Discontents,* trans. James Strachey (New York: W. W. Norton & Co., 1962), p. 39.
25. Claude Lévi-Strauss, *The Savage Mind,* trans. George Weidenfield and Nicolson Ltd. (Chicago: The University of Chicago Press, 1966), pp. 16–19.
26. Joseph Needham, *Science and Civilization in China* (Cambridge: Cambridge University Press, 1971), 4:7, pp. 418–20.
27. For a discussion of the relics and their interpretation as the "cult of the ship," see Max Raphael, *Prehistoric Pottery and Civilization in Egypt,* trans. Norbert Guterman (New York: Bollingen Foundation, 1947), pp. 136–37, 141–43.
28. José Ortega y Gasset, *An Interpretation of Universal History,* trans. Mildred Adams. (New York: W. W. Norton & Co., 1973), p. 73. For a semiotic interplay between economics and esthetics via the opportunity of ships, see my "Aesthetics of British Mercantilism," *New Literary History* 11 (Winter 1980):303–21.
29. For a discussion see Karl R. Popper, *Conjectures and Refutations: The Growth of Scientific Knowledge* (New York: Harper Torchbooks, 1962), p. 138.
30. George Thomson, *Studies in Greek Philosophy: The Greek Philosophers,* (New York: Citadel Press, 1965) 2:159.

31. See Raymond Williams, *Culture and Society 1780–1950* (New York: Harper Torchbooks, 1958), p. 219.

32. For a critique of instrumentalism see Popper, *Conjectures and Refutations,* Chapter 3.

33. John Dewey, *Art as Experience* (New York: Capricorn Books, 1958), "The Act of Expression," p. 64.

34. Charles Morris, *Foundations of the Theory of Signs* (Chicago: The University of Chicago Press, 1938). For a discussion see Umberto Eco, *A Theory of Semiotics* (Bloomington: Indiana University Press, 1976), p. 16.

35. Herman Von Helmholtz, *Popular Scientific Lectures,* trans. H. W. Eve (New York: Dover Publications, 1962), p. 5.

36. Plutarch, *The Lives of the Noble Grecians and Romans,* trans. John Dryden (New York: Modern Library, 1932), p. 186.

37. Arturo Rosenbluth and Norbert Wiener, "The Role of Models in Science," *Philosophy of Science* 12 (1945):316.

38. Herbert A. Snow, "The Architecture of Complexity," *Proceedings of the American Philosophical Society* 106 (December 1962):479.

39. Ogden & Richards, p. 11.

40. Eco, pp. 56–57.

41. Martin Gardner, *The Ambidextrous Universe: Left, Right, and the Fall of Parity* (New York: Mentor Books, 1969), p. 153.

42. Erwin Panofsky, *Galileo as a Critic of the Arts* (The Hague: Martinus Nijhof, 1954), pp. 9–10.

43. J. Z. Young, *An Introduction to the Study of Man* (Oxford: Oxford University Press, 1971), p. 46.

Chapter 1

1. J. Bronowski, *The Ascent of Man* (Boston: Little, Brown & Co., 1973), p. 24. I am indebted to his chapter, "The Grain in the Stone," for the important distinction between the hand's analytic as averse to its moulding capacities.

2. Michael Polanyi, "Knowing and Being," collected in *Knowing and Being: Essays by Michael Polanyi,* ed. Marjorie Grene (Chicago: University of Chicago Press, 1969), p. 125.

3. Sigfried Giedion, *The Eternal Present: The Beginnings of Art* (New York: Bollingen Foundation, 1962), pp. 93–100.

4. Max Raphael, *Prehistoric Cave Paintings,* trans. Norbert Guterman (New York: Bollingen Foundation, 1945), pp. 20–37.

5. J. Z. Young, *An Introduction to the Study of Man* (New York: Oxford University Press, 1971), p. 486.

6. Martin Gardner, *The Ambidextrous Universe* (New York: Mentor, 1969), Chapters 4, 22.

7. Joseph Needham, *Science and Civilization in China* (Cambridge: Cambridge University Press, 1954–), 2:45–46.

8. Cited by Alfred North Whitehead, *Religion in the Making* (New York: Macmillan Co., 1926), p. 74.

9. Rousseau, *Emile,* trans. Barbara Foxley (New York: E. P. Dutton, 1961), p. 151.

10. Giedion, p. 79.

11. Young, pp. 486–87.

12. Stuart Mosher, *The Story of Money, Bulletin of the Buffalo Society of Natural Sciences,* vol. 27, no. 2 (1936), p. 21.

13. Niels Bohr, *Atomic Theory and the Description of Nature* (Cambridge: Cambridge Univeristy Press, 1934), p. 99. For an overview of Bohr see Gerald Holton, "The Roots of Complementarity," in *Thematic Origins of Scientific Thought: Kepler to Einstein* (Cambridge, Mass.: Harvard University Press, 1973), pp. 115–61. See also Holton's "Conveying Science by Visual Presentation," in *Education of Vision,* ed. Gyorgy Kepes (New York: G. Braziller, 1965), pp. 50–77, for an argument favoring the unsanitized reality of actual laboratory demonstration.

14. Polanyi, p. 127.

15. For a discussion of the pointing hand see Umberto Eco, *A Theory of Semiotics* (Bloomington: Indiana University Press, 1976), pp. 115–21. See also K. T. Fann, *Wittgenstein's Conception of Philosophy* (Berkeley: University of California Press, 1969), p. 74.

16. See Ernst Cassirer, *An Essay on Man* (New Haven: Yale University Press, 1944), p. 206.

17. Martin Heidegger, *An Introduction to Metaphysics,* trans. Ralph Manheim (New Haven: Yale University Press, 1959), p. 1–3.

18. See Roman Jakobson, "A Few Remarks on Peirce, Pathfinder in the Science of Language," *Modern Language Notes* 92 (December 1977): 1029–030, for invariance.

19. Emmon Bach, "Structural Linguistics and the Philosophy of Science," *Diogenes* 51 (Fall 1965): 111–28.

20. Raphael, p. 57.

21. See Giedion's Conclusion, "The Space Conception of Prehistory," 1:513–38.

22. See Peter Tompkins, *Secrets of the Great Pyramid* (New York: Harper and Row, 1971), p. 46. For an introduction to pyramidal mathematics, see Lancelot Hogben, *Science for the Citizen* (London: George Allen & Unwin Ltd., 1940), Chapter 1, "Pole Star and Pyramid."

23. Arthur H. Robinson and Barbara Bartz Petchenik, *The Nature of Maps* (Chicago: The University of Chicago Press, 1976), p. 14.

24. Claude Lévi-Strauss, "Split Representation in the Art of Asia and America," in *Structural Anthropology*, trans. Claire Jacobson and Brooke Grundfest Schoepf (Garden City: Anchor Books, 1967), pp. 260–61.

25. Thomas Hobbes, *Leviathan*, ed. A. R. Waller (Cambridge: Cambridge University Press, 1935), p. 9.

26. Young, pp. 516, 46–50.

27. For a discussion see Gerald M. Weinberg, *An Introduction to General Systems Thinking* (New York: John Wiley and Sons, 1975), pp. 87–94.

28. Jean Piaget, *Genetic Epistemology*, trans. Eleanor Duckworth (New York: W. W. Norton & Co., 1970), p. 43. For a good textbook based on Piaget's topological theory, see David J. Fuys and Rosamund Welchman Tischler, *Teaching Mathematics in the Elementary School* (Boston: Little, Brown & Co., 1979).

29. James D. Watson, *The Double Helix: A Personal Account of the Discovery of the Structure of DNA* (New York: Signet, 1969), p. 136.

30. Thomas A. Sebeok, "Goals and Limitations of the Study of Animal Communication," in *Animal Communication*, ed. Thomas A. Sebeok (Bloomington: Indiana University Press, 1968), p. 12. For a discussion of the role of genetic information within the general system of cellular communication, see Gunther S. Stent, "Cellular Communication," in *Communication*, (San Francisco: W. H. Freeman & Co., 1972), pp. 17–25.

31. Young, p. 47.

32. See Gardner, Chapters 12, 13, 14 for a discussion of the handedness of carbon molecules, the conventions of describing two-dimensional and three-dimensional chemical models, and the structure of DNA.

33. John Dewey, *Art as Experience* (New York: Putnam Capricorn, 1958), Chapter 8, "The Organization of Energies." See also James Bunn, "Circle and Sequence in the Conjectural Lyric," *New Literary History* 3 (1971–1972):511–26, for a discussion of Dewey's ideas about rhythm.

34. Henri Bergson, *Creative Evolution*, trans. Arthur Mitchell (New York: Modern Library, 1944), p. 328.

35. Jean Piaget and Barbara Inhelder, *The Child's Conception of Space*, trans. F. J. Langdon and J. L. Lunzer (New York: W. W. Norton & Co., 1967), Chapter 4, "The Study of Knots and the Relationship of 'Surrounding.' " For a recent discussion of topology and knotting, see Lee Neuwirth, "The Theory of Knots," *Scientific American*, vol. 240, June 1979, pp. 110–24.

36. See Jane S. Richardson, "B-Sheet Topology and the Relatedness of Proteins," *Nature*, vol. 268, 11 August 1977, pp. 495–500.

37. Johann Wolfgang von Goethe, *Italian Journey 1786–1788*, trans. W. H. Auden and Elizabeth Mayer (New York: Schocken, 1968), pp. 401–02.

38. See A. H. Church, *The Relation of Phyllotaxis to Mechanical Law* (London: Williams and Norgate, 1904), p. 1. Cited by H. S. M. Coxeter, *Introduction to Geometry,* 2d ed. (New York: John Wiley & Sons, Inc., 1969), p. 169.

Chapter 2

1. Bertram D. Lewin, *The Image and the Past* (New York: International Universities Press, 1968), pp. 33–41.
2. Rudolph E. Heyman, "An Approach to Early Art through Technical Drawing," *Proceedings of the Tenth International Congress of the History of Science* (Paris: 1964), pp. 373–75.
3. Frances Yates, *The Art of Memory* (Chicago: The University of Chicago Press, 1966).
4. Rudolph Arnheim, *Visual Thinking* (Berkeley: University of California Press, 1969), p. 137.
5. P. W. Bridgman, *The Way Things Are* (Cambridge, Mass.: Harvard University Press, 1959), p. 34.
6. Karl R. Popper, "Back to the Presocratics," in *Conjectures and Refutations,* (New York: Harper Torchbooks, 1965), pp. 136–65.
7. I. J. Gelb, *A Study of Writing* (Chicago: The University of Chicago Press, 1963), p. 12.
8. Denise Schmandt-Besserat, "An Archaic Recording System and the Origin of Writing," *Syro-Mesopotamian Studies* 1 (July 1977):31–70.
9. Charles H. Kahn, *Anaximander and the Origin of Greek Cosmology* (New York: Columbia University Press, 1960), p. 82.
10. Popper, p. 139.
11. Lancelot Hogben, *Science for the Citizen* (London: George Allen & Unwin Ltd., 1938; 1966), p. 105. Also Joseph Needham, *Science and Civilization in China* (Cambridge: Cambridge University Press, 1954–), 1:231 for a simultaneous appearance in China.
12. Hogben, p. 74.
13. J. Z. Young, *An Introduction to the Study of Man* (New York: Oxford University Press, 1971), p. 497.
14. Cited by Arnheim, "Models for Theory," a chapter from which many of my conjectures derive.
15. Cited by Alexander Koyré, *From the Closed World to the Infinite Universe* (Baltimore: The Johns Hopkins University Press, 1957), p. 117.
16. See Walter J. Ong, "System, Space and Intellect in Renaissance Symbolism," collected in *The Barbarian Within and Other Fugitive Essays* (New York: Macmillan, 1962).

17. For a discussion, see Erwin Panofsky, *Albrecht Dürer* (Princeton: Princeton University Press, 1945). The Chapter "Dürer as a Mathematician," is in James R. Newman's four-volume anthology *The World of Mathematics* (New York: Simon & Schuster, 1956), 1:603–21. See also Ernst H. Gombrich, *Art and Illusion: A Psychology of Pictorial Representation* (Princeton: Bollingen Foundation, 1961), p. 306.

18. See Morris Kline, *Mathematical Thought from Ancient to Modern Times* (New York: Oxford University Press, 1972), pp. 308–19, and Lancelot Hogben, *Mathematics for the Millions* (New York: W. W. Norton & Co., 1964), p. 346.

19. For Mario Praz, this is a typical Mannerist painting. See *Mnemosyne: The Parallel between Literature and the Visual Arts* (Princeton: Bollingen Foundation, 1967), p. 93.

20. Marshall McLuhan and Harley Parker, *Through the Vanishing Point: Space in Poetry and Painting* (New York: Harper Colophon Books, 1968), p. 55.

21. Kline, p. 302.

22. See Kline, pp. 320–21, for three-dimensional coordinate geometry. See Gerald Holton, *Thematic Origins of Scientific Thought: Kepler to Einstein* (Cambridge: Harvard University Press, 1973), pp. 25–26, 53–60, for a model of scientific analysis that uses three-dimensional coordinates.

23. See Panofsky, p. 675.

24. Richard Courant and Herbert Robbins, "Euler's Formula for Polyhedra," *What is Mathematics?* (Oxford: Oxford University Press, 1941), in Newman, 1:581.

25. Franz Boas, *Primitive Art* (New York: Dover Publications, 1955), p. 223. See also Claude Lévi-Strauss, "Split Representation in the Art of Asia and America," in *Structural Anthropology*, trans. Claire Jacobson and Brooke Grundfest Schoepf (New York: Anchor, 1967), pp. 245–68.

26. See Erwin Panofsky, *Galileo as a Critic of the Arts* (The Hague: Martinus Nijhof, 1954), pp. 13–16.

27. D'Arcy Wentworth Thompson, *On Growth and Form*, ed. J. T. Bonner, abridged ed. (Cambridge: Cambridge University Press, 1961). See also Stephen Jay Gould, "D'Arcy Thompson and the Science of Form," *New Literary History* 2 (Winter 1971).

28. Ludwig Wittgenstein, *Tractatus Logico-Philosophicus* (London: Routledge & Kegan Paul, 1922), p. 177.

29. Bertrand Russell, *The ABC of Relativity*, ed. Felix Pirani, 3d rev. ed. (London: Signet, 1969), pp. 79–81.

30. A related phenomenon in contemporary diagrammatics is René Thom's catastrophe theory. See E. C. Zeeman, "Catastrophe Theory," *Scientific American* 234 (April 1976):65–83.

31. For a useful compilation of Peirce's disparate writings about the trichotomy of signs into icon, index, and symbol, see *Philosophical Writings of Peirce* (New York: Dover Publications, 1955), pp. 98–119.
32. James J. Gi¹ ;on, *The Perception of the Visual World* (Boston: Houghton Mifflin, 1950). His distinction has been useful to Rudolph Arnheim, *Art and Visual Perception: A Psychology of the Creative Eye,* rev. ed. (Berkeley: University of California Press, 1974), to Gombrich, and to Wylie Sypher, *Literature and Technology: The Alien Vision* (New York: Vintage Books, 1968). See especially Don Ihde, *Experimental Phenomenology: An Introduction* (New York: Capricorn Books, 1977), Chapter 3.
33. See E. H. Gombrich, "The Visual Image" in *Communication* (San Francisco: W. H. Freeman, 1972), pp. 46–62.
34. Arnheim, *Visual Thinking,* p. 231.
35. For a different perspective on binary thinking, see Philip Morrison, "The Modularity of Knowing," in *Module, Proportion, Symmetry, Rhythm,* ed. Gyorgy Kepes (New York: G. Braziller, 1966). pp. 1–19.
36. See F. Vaihinger, *The Philosophy of "As If": A System of the Practical and Religious Features of Mankind,* trans. C. K. Ogden (New York: Harcourt, Brace & Co., 1924), pp. 179–82.

Chapter 3

1. See Theodore Mommsen, *Corpus Inscriptionuua Latinarum* (Berlin: Apud Weidmannos, 1918), vol. 1, parts 1 and 2.
2. Most of my discussion of time's arrow is drawn from C. J. Whitrow, *The Natural Philosophy of Time* (London: Thomas Nelson, 1961), and his *Nature of Time* (Baltimore: Penguin Books, 1975).
3. Whitrow, *Nature of Time,* pp. 123, 135.
4. Ibid., p. 135.
5. Whitrow, *Natural Philosophy of Time,* pp. 74–75.
6. Ibid., pp. 228, 293.
7. Cited by Roman Jakobson, "Quest for the Essence of Language," *Diogenes* 51 (Fall 1965): 36–37. From Peirce's *Existential Graphs,* 4:360.
8. Whitrow, *Natural Philosophy of Time,* pp. 295–96.
9. Michael Polanyi, *Personal Knowledge: Towards a Post-Critical Philosophy* (Harper Torchbooks, 1964), pp. 393–402.
10. Umberto Eco, *A Theory of Semiotics* (Bloomington: Indiana University Press, 1976), pp. 68–72.
11. Whitrow, *Nature of Time,* p. 29.
12. Bertrand de Jouvenal, *The Art of Conjecture,* trans. Nikita Lary (New York: Basic Books, 1967), p. 27.

13. For example, see "An American Indian Model of the Universe," collected in *Language, Thought and Reality: Selected Writings of Benjamin Lee Whorf,* ed. John B. Carroll (Cambridge, Mass.: The M.I.T. Press, 1956). For an overview of tense and time in different languages, see John B. Lyons, *Introduction to Theoretical Linguistics* (Cambridge, Mass.: Cambridge University Press, 1968), pp. 304–06.

14. Alfred North Whitehead, *Science and the Modern World* (New York: Macmillan, 1925; 1953), p. 24.

15. Karl Menninger, *Number Words and Number Symbols: A Cultural History of Numbers,* trans. Paul Broneer (Cambridge, Mass.: The M.I.T. Press, 1969). For his discussion of tally sticks, to which this section is indebted, see pp. 223–51.

16. Alexander Marshack, *The Roots of Civilization: The Cognitive Beginnings of Man's First Art, Symbol and Notation* (New York: McGraw-Hill, 1972).

17. Morris Kline, *Mathematical Thought from Ancient to Modern Times* (New York: Oxford University Press, 1972), pp. 1199–201.

18. Whitehead, p. 27.

19. *The Born-Einstein Letters: Correspondence between Albert Einstein and Max and Hedwig Born, From 1916–1945* (New York: Walker and Co., 1971), p. 95.

20. Lancelot Hogben, *Mathematics for the Million* (New York: W. W. Norton, 1968), p. 40.

21. For a discussion of Newton's attitude toward these mysteries, see Frank Manuel, *A Portrait of Newton* (Cambridge, Mass.: Harvard University Press, 1968), pp. 391, 467. For an excellent analysis of Newton's beliefs in this regard, springing from the tradition of Cambridge Platonism, see J. E. McQuire and P. M. Rattansi, "Newton and the 'Pipes of Pan,'" *Notes and Records of the Royal Society of London* 21 (1966): 108–43.

22. Bertrand Russell, *The ABC of Relativity* (New York: Signet, 1956), p. 63.

23. James R. Newman, *The World of Mathematics* (New York: Simon and Schuster, 1956), 1:80. See also Russell, p. 63, for the rule of thumb about 3–4–5 units of length. See also, Hogben, pp. 47–48. See also Joseph Needham, *Science and Civilization in China* (Cambridge: Cambridge University Press, 1954–), 4:167–213, for an extensive comparison of Pythagorean and Chinese harmonics.

24. For an overview, see Edward A. Lippman, *Musical Thought in Ancient Greece* (New York: Columbia University Press, 1964). Also Isabel Henderson, "Ancient Greek Music," in *New Oxford History of Music: Ancient and Oriental Music* (London: Oxford University Press, 1957), 1:341ff.

25. Kline, p. 148.

26. Lippman, p. 136.

27. The sketch of nodes, fingers, and vibrating strings—but not the triangular conjecture—has been adopted from a vivid photograph in Jacob Bronowski's *The Ascent of Man* (Boston: Little, Brown, 1973), p. 154.

28. For an introduction to the rationale of Pythagorean cosmology, see Milton C. Nahm, *Selections from Early Greek Philosophy* (New York: Appleton-Century-Crofts, 1934), pp. 5–52; and almost any scholarly edition of Plato's *Timaeus* includes at least a brief discussion of the *tetractys* and Plato's "soul stuff."

29. Needham, pp. 178–80.

30. McGuire and Rattansi, p. 115.

31. P. W. Bridgman, *Dimensional Analysis,* rev. ed. (New Haven: Yale University Press, 1937), p. 154. Einstein often wrote about logical errors regarding time. See Gerald Holton, "Constructing a Theory: Einstein's Model," *American Scholar* (Summer, 1979), 309–40, but especially, 315–17.

32. Whitehead, pp. 49–51, 55, 58–59, 144–48. This 'orthodox' view was not unchallenged in the seventeenth and eighteenth centuries. See, for instance, Henry More's argument with Descartes about the latter's stipulation that mind exists, but not in space, summarized in Alexander Koyré, *From the Closed World to the Infinite Universe* (Baltimore: Johns Hopkins University Press, 1957), Chapter 5; also in Basil Willey, *The Seventeenth-Century Background: The Thought of the Age in Relation to Religion and Poetry* (New York: Doubleday Anchor, 1934), Chapter 8. Both are indebted to E. A. Burtt's "Conclusion" to *The Metaphysical Foundations of Modern Physical Science* (New York: Doubleday Anchor, 1924; 1932). For a discussion of the pernicious mis-influence of the phrase "in the mind," see Isaiah Berlin, *The Age of Enlightenment* (New York: Mentor Books, 1956), "Introduction," and commentary upon David Hume. Karl R. Popper calls this kind of container a "bucket" theory of mentation, in *The Open Society and its Enemies,* 3d ed. (Princeton: Princeton University Press, 1957), 2:213– .

33. Whitrow, *Natural Philosophy,* p. 113.

Chapter 4

1. See Gunther S. Stent, "Cellular Communication," in *Communication* (San Francisco: W. H. Freeman, 1972), pp. 17–25.

2. Morton Bloomfield, "The Study of Language," *Daedalus* 102, no. 9 (Summer 1973), p. 9.

3. Ferdinand de Saussure, *Course in General Linguistics,* ed. Charles Bally et al., trans. Wade Baskin (New York: McGraw-Hill, 1966), Chapter 3.

For an authoritative overview of twentieth-century linguistics, with Saus-
sure at its center, see Roman Jakobson, *Main Trends in the Science of
Language* (New York: Harper Torchbooks, 1973), Chapter 1, "Linguistic
Vistas."

4. G. J. Whitrow, *The Natural Philosophy of Time* (London: Thomas Nel-
son, 1961), p. 153. Furthermore, a historical sketch of the idea of space-
time, indeed, the very notion of four-dimensional thinking, would be
inadequate without reference to Hermann Minkowski. See Peter Louis
Galison's essay about discovery, "Minkowski's Space-Time: From Visual
Thinking to the Absolute World," in *Historical Studies in the Physical
Sciences,* eds. Russell McCormach, Lewis Pyenson, and Roy Steven
Turner (Baltimore: Johns Hopkins University Press, 1979), pp. 85–121.

5. Roman Jakobson, "Verbal Communication," in *Communication,* pp.
39–42.

6. Jakobson cites Gerald Holton's work about Einstein. See his *Thematic
Origins of Modern Science* (Cambridge, Mass.: Harvard University Press,
1973), Chapters 5–10.

7. Jean Piaget, *Structuralism,* trans. Chaninah Maschler (New York: Basic Books, 1970), p. 54.

8. Kurt Koffka, *Principles of Gestalt Psychology* (New York: Harbinger
Book, 1935), p. 41.

9. See C. H. Waddington, *Behind Appearances, A Study of the Relations
between Painting and the Natural Sciences in this Century* (Cambridge, Mass.:
M.I.T. Press, 1969).

10. Piaget, pp. 13–16.

11. Johannes von Uexküll, *Theoretical Biology* (New York: Harcourt,
Brace & Co., 1926). Cited by Ernst Cassirer, *An Essay on Man,* (New
Haven: Yale University Press, 1944), pp. 23–24.

12. Ludwig von Bertalanffy, *General System Theory: Foundations, Develop-
ments, Applications* (New York: George Braziller, 1968), pp. 10–17. But
see also Piaget's *Structuralism,* pp. 44–48. A good introduction is Weinberg's *An Introduction to General System Theory* (New York: John Wiley &
Sons, 1975). For the importance of Whitehead's concept of "organization," see Waddington, pp. 109–15.

13. Francois Jacob, *The Logic of Life: A History of Heredity,* trans. Betty E.
Spillman (New York: Pantheon, 1973), p. 190. All of Chapter 2, on
"Organization," is valuable for its historical overview.

14. Perhaps the most thorough recent survey of Romantic thought is M.
H. Abrams, *Natural Supernaturalism: Tradition and Revolt in Romantic Literature* (New York: W. W. Norton & Co., 1971). For a discussion of a
Romantic philosophy based on the metaphor of the flower, see Abrams,
pp. 431–62.

15. Goethe, *Italian Journey 1786–1788*, trans. W. H. Auden and Elizabeth Mayer (New York: Schocken, 1968), pp. 251–52.
16. Stephen Jay Gould, "Evolutionary Paleontology and the Science of Form," *Earth-Science Reviews* 6 (1970):97.
17. This discussion of Schlegel is taken from Thomas A. Sebeok, "Goals and Limitations of the Study of Animal Communication," in *Animal Communication: Techniques of Study and Results of Research,* ed. Thomas A. Sebeok (Bloomington: Indiana University Press, 1968), p. 4. See especially Noam Chomsky, *Cartesian Linguistics: A Chapter in the History of Rationalist Thought* (New York: Harper & Row, 1966), pp. 19–31 for an insightful study of Schlegel and Goethe as generative grammarians from an "Urform." The new wave of variation-invariance in turn-of-the-century mathematics may have sprung from a commonplace of Romantic organicism.
18. Ann Harleman Stewart, *Graphic Representation of Models in Linguistic Theory* (Bloomington: Indiana University Press, 1976). Chapter 1 is called "Tree Models."
19. Arthur Koestler, "Beyond Atomism and Holism—the Concept of the Holon," in *Beyond Reductionism: New Perspectives in the Life Sciences,* ed. Arthur Koestler and A. R. Smythies (Boston: Hutchinson Publishing Group, 1969), p. 193.
20. D'Arcy Thompson, *On Growth and Form,* ed. John Tyler Bonner, abridged ed. (Cambridge University Press, 1969), p. 61.
21. Gyorgy Kepes, *Arts of the Environment* (New York: George Braziller, 1972), p. 3.
22. José Ortega y Gasset, *An Interpretation of Universal History* (New York: W. W. Norton Co., 1973), p. 35.
23. See Robert S. Brumbaugh, *Ancient Greek Gadgets and Machines* (New York: Thomas Y. Crowell Co., 1966), Chapter 4, "Scientists and Model Makers."
24. Joseph Needham, *Science and Civilization in China* (Cambridge: Cambridge University Press, 1954–), 2:125.
25. Lynn White, Jr., "Technology and Invention in the Middle Ages," *Speculum* 15(April 1940):153.
26. The following discussion is taken from H. W. Dickinson, *James Watt, Craftsman and Engineer* (Cambridge: Cambridge University Press, 1936).
27. Sebeok, p. 12.
28. For a running attack on reductionism, see Koestler and Smythies.
29. See Jacques Monod, *Chance and Necessity: An Essay on the Natural Philosophy of Modern Biology* (New York: Alfred A. Knopf, 1971), pp. 79–80.
30. Jacob, pp. 7–8.

31. Thomas S. Kuhn, *The Logic of Scientific Discovery,* rev. ed. (Chicago: The University of Chicago Press, 1970), the section on "Normal Science."

32. Piaget, p. 34.

33. John Dewey, *Art as Experience* (New York: Capricorn Books, 1958), p. 169.

Conclusion

1. John Locke, *An Essay Concerning Human Understanding,* ed. Peter H. Nidditch (Oxford: Oxford University Press, 1975), Book 2, p. 204. For a commentary about the modernism of the passage, see G. J. Whitrow, *Natural Philosophy of Time* (London: Thomas Nelson, 1961), p. 223.

2. E. J. Hobsbawm, *The Age of Revolution 1789–1848* (New York: Mentor, 1962), pp. 45–46.

3. Frank E. Manuel, *The Age of Reason* (Ithaca: Cornell University Press, 1951), p. 74. See also Jacques Ellul, *The Technological Society,* trans. John Wilkinson (New York: Vintage, 1964), pp. 87–92, where technical innovations augment one another in a geometrical progression, i.e., "acceleration," p. 421.

4. Henry Adams, *The Education of Henry Adams* (New York: Modern Library, 1931); *The Degradation of the Democratic Dogma* (New York: MacMillan, 1920); and Brooks Adams, *The Law of Civilization and Decay: An Essay on History* (1896; New York: Alfred Knopf, 1943).

5. See Henry Adams' chapter "The Rule of Phase Applied to History," *Degradation*, p. 308. Gerald Piel cites this passage in *The Acceleration of History* (New York: Alfred Knopf, 1972), p. 23. He diagrams a number of exponential curves that mirror an end of economic abandon in an era of accelerating complexity. For a similar meditation, beginning with Adams, see Gunther S. Stent, *Paradoxes of Progress* (San Francisco: W. H. Freeman & Co., 1978), Chapter 1, "The Ends of Progress."

6. Manuel, p. 80.

7. Albert Einstein, "Morals and Emotions," in *Out of My Later Years* (New York: Littlefield, Adams & Co., 1950), p. 21.

8. Ernst Cassirer, *An Essay on Man* (New Haven: Yale University Press, 1944), p. 25.

9. See Bertrand de Jouvenal, "Rousseau's Theory of Government," in *Hobbes and Rousseau: A Collection of Critical Essays,* ed. Maurice Cranston and Richard S. Peters (Garden City, N.Y.: Anchor, 1972), pp. 484–97. For a discussion of the metaphor of balance and mixed forms of government with respect to British historiography, see my "The Tory View of Geography," *Boundary 2,* vol. 7, no. 2 (Winter 1979), pp. 149–67.

10. Rousseau, *The Social Contract,* Book 3, Chapter 1; cited by Jouvenal, p. 492.

11. Rousseau, *Letters from the Mountain;* cited by Jouvenal, p. 495.

12. See *An Essay on the Principle of Population,* ed. Philip Appleman (New York: Norton Critical Edition, 1976).

13. D'Arcy Wentworth Thomson, *On Growth and Form,* abridged ed., ed. John Tyler Bonner (Cambridge: Cambridge University Press, 1961), p. 35.

14. Henry Adams, *Degradation,* pp. 306–07.

15. Martin Heidegger, *An Introduction to Metaphysics,* trans. Ralph Manheim (Garden City, N.Y.: Anchor, 1961).

16. Hannah Arendt, *The Human Condition* (Chicago: The University of Chicago Press, 1958), p. 102.

17. Edward O. Wilson, *On Human Nature* (Cambridge, Mass: Harvard University Press, 1978), "Glossary."

18. Paul Garvin, "Linguistics and Semiotics," *Semiotica* 20 1/2(1977): 106.

19. Jouvenal, *Art of Conjecture,* pp. 93–95.

20. Stent, p. 52.

21. Morris Kline, *Mathematical Thought from Ancient to Modern Times* (New York: Oxford University Press, 1973), p. 33. See also Cassirer, p. 212.

22. Raymond Williams, *Keywords: A Vocabulary of Culture and Society* (New York: Oxford University Press, 1976), p. 29. See also "In Praise of Alienation," Chapter 1 of Herbert N. Schneidau's *Sacred Discontent: The Bible and the Western Tradition* (Baton Rouge: Louisiana State University Press, 1976).

23. Isaiah Berlin, *Karl Marx: His Life and Environment* (New York: Oxford University Press, 1939; 1963), pp. 137–38.

24. Arendt, pp. 102, 137.

25. "Reification" is the term used by Georg Lukacs in order to translate Marx's phrase "commodity fetishism," in *History and Class Consciousness: Studies in Marxist Dialectics,* trans. Rodney Livingston (Cambridge, Mass.: M.I.T. Press, 1971); see the chapter "Reification and the Consciousness of the Proletariat," pp. 83–222. For a discussion, see Lucien Goldmann, *Lukacs and Heidegger: Towards a New Philosophy,* trans. William Q. Boelhower (London: Routledge & Kegan Paul, 1977), pp. 27–29.

26. Wylie Sypher, *Literature and Technology: The Alien Vision* (New York: Vintage, 1968), pp. 196–97.

27. *Selections from Early Greek Philosophy,* trans. Milton C. Nahm (New York: Appleton-Century-Crofts, 1934; 1964), p. 281. For a discussion of suitability with respect to Greek thought, see Wladyslaw Tatarkiewicz, *History of Aesthetics,* vol. 1, *Ancient Aesthetics,* trans. Adam and Ann Czerniawski (The Hague: Mouton, 1970), pp. 95–102.

28. Einstein, p. 27.

29. For a discussion of the work of art removed from its originating context, see my "Aesthetics of British Mercantilism," *New Literary History* 11 (Winter 1980).

30. Ralph Waldo Emerson, "Thoreau," in *Lectures and Biographical Sketches* (Boston: Houghton, Mifflin & Co., 1904), 10:464.

31. Herman Melville, *Moby-Dick, or, The Whale* (New York: W. W. Norton & Co., 1967), "The Carpenter," pp. 458–59.

INDEX

199